Toasts

And Forms of Public Address for Those Who Wish to Say the Right Thing in the Right Way

William Pittenger

Alpha Editions

This edition published in 2023

ISBN : 9789362095916

Design and Setting By
Alpha Editions
www.alphaedis.com
Email - info@alphaedis.com

Contents

INTRODUCTION

The author of this manual has at various intervals prepared several treatises relating to the art of speech. Their wide circulation is an indication of the demand for works upon this subject. They were intended to embrace the principles which govern speech-making in the forum, in the pulpit, or at the bar. While these do not differ essentially from the principles applicable to occasions where the object is only entertainment, yet there are certain well-defined differences which it is the purpose of this little volume to point out. We hope thus to render the same service to a person who is called upon to offer or respond to a toast in a convivial assembly, as the author's previous volumes rendered to those preparing to speak upon subjects of a serious and practical nature.

That help is needed, and may be afforded, no one will deny. A novice called upon to participate in the exercises of a public banquet, an anniversary, or other entertainment, unless he has an experienced friend to give him a few hints or advice, is apt to be dismayed. He does not even know how to make a start in the work of preparation, and his sense of inability and fear of blundering go far to confuse and paralyze whatever native faculty he may have. A book like this comes to him at such a time as reinforcements to a sorely pressed army in the very crisis of a battle. As he reads, some ideas which seem practical, flash upon him. He learns what others before him have done. If he is to offer a toast, he examines the list furnished in this volume, finding one perhaps that pleases him, or one is suggested which is better adapted to his purpose than any in the book, and he wonders at the stupidity of the author in omitting it. Soon he becomes quite interested in this suggested toast, and compares it with those in the list to find out wherein it differs. Thus gradually and unconsciously he has prepared himself for the part he is to perform.

Or if invited to respond to a toast, he passes through a similar experience. He may find the outline of a speech on that very topic; he either uses it as it is printed or makes an effort to improve it by abridgment or enlargement. Next he looks through the treasury of anecdotes, selects one, or calls to mind one he has read elsewhere which he considers better. He then studies both of them in their bearings on the subject upon which he is to speak, and longs for the hour to arrive, when he will surprise and delight his friends by his performance. He rises to speak conscious that he knows a great deal, not only about the toast assigned to him, but about other toasts as well—feels that he has something to say which, at least, will fill in the time, and save him from confusion and discredit. He even hopes to win applause by means of the stories and happy turns with which his speech is interspersed.

He has thus satisfactorily taken the first step toward becoming a ready and entertaining after-dinner speaker. The sense of knowing how to do what is expected of him has a wonderfully quieting effect upon his nerves; and thus the study of this book will greatly add to the confidence of a speaker, and the effectiveness of his delivery. Whatever graces of manner he possesses will become available, instead of being subverted by an overmastering fear.

It is not easy to mention all the uses of such a manual. One who has been accustomed to speaking, but fears he is getting into a rut, can turn to this text-book and find something which is *not* so distressingly his own, that his friends expect him to parade it before them on all occasions.

He may glance over the outline of a speech altogether new and strange to him, and endeavor to adapt it to his own use; or he may weave together fragments of several speeches, or take the framework of one and construct upon it a speech which will enable him to make a new departure. A writer sometimes, after years of practice, finds it difficult to begin the composition of some simple reception or commemorative address; but the reading of a meagre outline, not one word or idea of which may be directly used, serves to break the spell of intellectual sloth or inertia, and starts him upon his work briskly and hopefully.

The field covered by the present volume is not entirely unoccupied. One of the earliest publications in this line is an anonymous English work, very dignified and conservative. The speeches it furnishes are painstaking, but a trifle heavy, and savor so much of English modes of expression, as well as thought and customs, as to be poorly adapted to this country. Two works have appeared in this country, also, one being intended apparently for wine parties only; the other, while containing a number of gem-like little speeches, fails to give the aid which is sought by the ordinary tyro, and is calculated rather to discourage him; giving him the impression that it is more difficult to become an acceptable after-dinner speaker than he had ever supposed. While a few of the best things in the latter volume are availed of, a different method is pursued in the present work. Outlines of speeches are preferred to those which are fully elaborated; and the few plain rules, by which a thing so informal and easy as an after-dinner speech may be produced, are so illustrated as to make their application almost a matter of course. Good-humor and brevity, an outline and a story—what more is needed, unless it be that serene self-confidence which enables a speaker to say even foolish and absurd things, with the assurance that all goes down at a public dinner? What if you are not the most brilliant, humorous, and stirring speaker of the evening? Aim to fill your place without discredit; observe closely those who make a great success; the next time you may have a better outline or more telling story, and become, before you know it, the leader of the evening.

It is not intended to give rules or directions for the order either of drinking or feasting. That field is fully occupied. But the custom of making addresses at the close of a feast has, been so thoroughly established, and so frequent are these occasions, that a gentleman is not fully equipped for a place in society, if he cannot gracefully offer or respond to a toast, or preside at a gathering where toasts or other forms of after-dinner speaking are expected. It is the aim of this manual to help the beginner in this field.

AFTER-DINNER SPEECHES—ANCIENT AND MODERN

An idea of the real meaning of after-dinner speaking may be obtained from the feudal feasts of earlier times. The old lord or baron of the Middle Ages partook of his principal meal in the great hall of his castle, surrounded by guests, each being assigned his place in formal order and with no small degree of ceremony. This hall was the main feature of the castle. There all the family and guests met on frequent festal occasions, and after the feasting and the hour of ceremony and more refined entertainment was over, retired to rest in comparatively small and humble apartments adjoining, though sometimes they would simply wrap their cloaks about them, and lie down to sleep on the rushes that littered the floor of the great hall.

After the "rage of hunger was appeased"—which then, as in our day, and back even as far as the time of the ancient Greeks, was the first business in order—came the social hour, which meant much to the dwellers in those dull, comfortless old barracks—for the great castles of that day were little better than barracks. The chief gave the signal for talk, music, or story, previous to which, any inquiries or conversation, other than the briefest question and answer about the food or other necessary things, would have been considered inappropriate and disrespectful. There probably was present some guest, who came under circumstances that awakened the strongest curiosity or who had a claim upon his entertainer. Such a guest was placed at the board in a position corresponding to his rank.

After resting and partaking of the repast, it was pertinent to hear what account he could give of himself, and courtesy permitted the host to levy an intellectual tax upon him, as a contribution to the joy of the hour. Seated at the head of the table the chief, or, in his absence, a representative, made the opening speech—the address of welcome, to use the term familiar to ourselves. This might be very brief or at considerable length; it might suggest inquiries of any of the company or merely pledge an attentive and courteous hearing to whatever the guest might utter; it might refer to the past glory of the castle and its lord, or vaunt its present greatness and active occupation.

But whatever form it might take it was sure to consist—as addresses of welcome in all ages have done—of two words, by dexterously using which, any man can make a good speech of this character. These two words are "We" and "You;" and all else not connected with these is irrelevant and useless. They do not constitute two parts of the same speech but ordinarily play back and forth, like a game of battledore. Who "we" are; what "we" have done; how "we" saw "you;" what "we" have heard of "you;" how great and good "you" are thought to be; the joy at "your" coming; what "we" now want to learn of "you;" what "we" wish "you" to do; how "we" desire a longer stay or regret the need of an early departure—all is a variation of the one theme— "we" and "you."

The old Baron probably said all of this and much more in a lordly way, occupying a longer or shorter time, without ever dreaming that he was making a speech. It was his ordinary after-dinner talk to those whom chance or fortune brought within his walls. Or, if he prided himself upon being a man of few words, scorning these as fit only for women and minstrels, he would simply remind the guest that he was now at liberty to give such an account of himself, and to prefer such requests as seemed agreeable to him.

The guest was then expected to respond, though this by no means was the rule. The host might wish first to call out more of his own intellectual treasures. This he would do by having other occupants of the castle speak further words of welcome, or would call upon a minstrel to sing a song or relate some deed of chivalry.

When the guest at last rises to speak, it is still the two pronouns with slightly changed emphasis that play a conspicuous part. The "we" may become "I;" but this is no essential change. Where "I" or "we" have been; what "I" have done, suffered, or enjoyed; how and why "I" came here; how glad "I" am to be here; what "I" have known and heard of "you;" how "we" may help each other; what great enterprises "we" can enter upon; how thankful for the good cheer and good words "we" hear.

In the baronial hall, which foreshadowed the family fireside of later days, the drinking was free and copious whilst the other portions of the entertainment were of a general character and quite protracted. Mirth, song, the rude jest, anecdotes of the chase or of a battle, or a rehearsal of the experiences of every-day life, were all in place. Sometimes, the guests, overpowered by their libations, are said to have fallen under the table and to have slumbered there till surprised by the pale morning light. There was little need of ceremony in such feasts, and there is little need of formality or constraint in the far different festal occasions of the present time.

When no guest, either by chance or invitation came to the castle, less variety could be given to the after-dinner entertainment, and many expedients were required to pass the long hours that sometimes hung heavily on their hands. Then the use of "Toasts" became an important feature. The drinking also was expected to arouse interest, but if it went on in silence and gloom or amid the buzz of trivial conversation in different parts of the hall the unity of the hour was marred and the evening was voted dull—the lord himself then having no more honor than his meanest vassal. But the toast—no matter how it originated—remedied all this. A compliment and a proverb, a speech and a response, however rude, fixed the attention of every one at the table, and enabled the lord to retain the same leadership at the feast that he had won in the chase or in battle. He might himself propose a toast of his own choice or give another permission to propose it. He might then designate some humorous or entertaining clansman to respond; he might either stimulate or repress the zeal of the guests, and give unity to each part of the entertainment and to the whole feast. For these reasons the toast rose into popularity, and is now often used—possibly it might be said generally used if our own country alone be considered—even when no drinking at all is indulged in.

Let us now take a look at an after-dinner hour of the present day; one of the very latest and most approved pattern. The contrast will not be without interest and value. The fare at the dinner is always inviting. The company is large. Good speakers are secured in advance. Each is given an appropriate toast, either to propose or respond to. Suppose it is a New England society celebrating Forefathers' Day in New York. The chairman (who is usually the president of the society) rises, and by touching a bell, rapping on the table, or in some other suitable manner, attracts all eyes to himself. He then asks the meeting to come to order, or if he prefers the form, to give attention. Then he utters a few graceful commonplaces, and calls upon a guest to offer the leading toast—not always the chief or most interesting one. When one is reached in which there is a lively interest, some distinguished person such as Chauncey M. Depew, the prince of after-dinner speakers, comes to the front. We give an outline of one of his addresses on Forefathers' Day, delivered December 22d, 1882, in response to the toast, "The Half Moon and the Mayflower."

In reading this address the "We" and "You" cannot fail to be noted. Mr. Depew said he did not know why he should be called upon to celebrate his conquerors. The Yankees had overcome the Dutch, and the two races are mingled. The speaker then introduced three fine stories—one at the expense of the Dutch who are slow in reaching their ends. A tenor singer at the church of a celebrated preacher said to Mr. Depew, "You must come again, the fact is the Doctor and myself were not at our best last Sunday morning." The second related to the inquisitiveness of a person who expressed himself thus to the guide upon the estate of the Duke of Westminster: "What, you can't tell how much the house cost or what the farm yields an acre, or what the old man's income is, or how much he is worth? Don't you Britishers know anything?" The third story, near the close, set off Yankee complacency. A New England girl mistook the first mile-stone from Boston for a tombstone, and reading its inscription "1 M. from Boston," said "I'm from Boston; how simple; how sufficient."

The serious part of the discourse was a rapid statement of the principles represented by the Dutch pioneer ship "Half Moon" and the Pilgrim

"Mayflower;" the elements of each contributed to national character and progress. (For speech in full see *Depew's Speeches*, Vol. I.)

Other toasts and responses followed; eloquence and humor mingled until the small hours of the night. Probably not one of that pleased and brilliant assemblage for a moment thought that they were doing at this anniversary what their old, barbaric ancestors did nightly, while resting after a border foray or Viking sea raid.

THE VALUE OF A GOOD STORY AND HOW TO INTRODUCE IT.

No matter how inexperienced a speaker may be or how stammering his utterance, if he can tell a good story, the average dinner party will pronounce him a success, and he will be able to resume his seat with a feeling of satisfaction. The efforts often made to bring in an entertaining story or a lively anecdote are sometimes quite amusing, but if they come in naturally the effect will unquestionably be happy. Almost any story, by using a little skill, can be adapted to nearly every occasion that may arise. We may mention a few among which a speaker can scarcely fail to find something to serve his purpose.

It is necessary always to be thoroughly familiar with the story and to understand its exact point. No matter how deliberately or with what difficulty you approach that part of your speech where the fun is to be introduced— yet, when that point *is* reached there must be no hesitation. It is well to memorize carefully the very words which express the pun, or the flash of wit or humor which is the climax of the story. The story itself may be found in such a manual as this, or in some volume of wit and humor.

There is no disadvantage in using wit gathered from any source, if it has not been so often used as to be completely worn out. When a good story is found anywhere and fully memorized and all its bearings and fine points thoroughly understood, there are two ways of getting it before an audience. The direct way is to say frankly that you have read a story and will tell it. This will answer very nicely when called upon for a speech. Few festive audiences are unwilling to accept a story for a speech, and a proposal to compromise on such terms is very likely in itself to bring applause. But the story in this case should be longer than if it is given as part of a speech. If, however, it should prove a failure, your performance will make a worse impression than when a poor story is introduced into a speech, although the story may only feebly illustrate any portion of it.

For these as well as other reasons most persons will prefer to make an address, even if it be very brief, and will endeavor to make the story fit into it. All stories that suggest diffidence, modesty, backwardness, or unwillingness to undertake great things, can be introduced to show how reluctant the speaker is to attempt a speech, and if these characteristics are only slightly referred to in the story it may still be used effectively and will leave a favorable impression.

If a topic, a toast, or a sentiment is given for a response, any of them may suggest a story; and after a good story has been told—one that has real point—it will be better to stop without making any attempt at application or explanation.

A great help is often found in the utterances of previous speakers. If these have done well, they may be complimented, and the compliment so contrived as to lead directly up to the story that is lying in wait; or something being said with which you heartily agree—however slight a portion of the address it may be—this harmony of views can be used in the same manner. On the other hand, if you disagree with any of the speakers, the mere reference to it will excite a lively interest. If this difference is used, not as the basis of a serious argument, but only to drag in a story illustrating the disagreement, the story will nevertheless appear to be very appropriate.

If you happen to be the first speaker, you are by no means without resources. You can then imagine what other speakers are going to say, and if you can slip in a humorous or good-natured hit at the expense of some of the prominent speakers, it will be, highly relished. If you describe what they are likely to say it will be enjoyed, while if you should happen to mention the very opposite this will be set down as your intention. You may even describe the different speakers, and be reminded of things that will bring in the prepared story very appropriately.

The writer once knew of a very dull speaker, who scored a great success in a popular meeting, by describing the eloquent speaker who was to follow. He began by telling how he was accustomed when a boy to take a skiff and follow in the wake of a steamer, to be rocked in its waves, but once getting before the huge vessel his boat was swept away, and he was nearly drowned. This unfortunately was his situation now, and he was in danger of being swept aside by the coming flood of eloquence. But he asked who is this coming man? It was the first time he had heard of him—then followed the story he had been trying to work in—a story wherein the eloquent man was described as "one who could give seventeen good reasons for anything under heaven." The story was a great success. In dumb show, the speaker he referred to begged for mercy. This only delighted the audience still more, and when the dull speaker finished it was admitted that, for once, he had escaped being stupid or commonplace. He had also forced upon the next speaker the necessity of removing the unpleasant effects of the jokes made at his expense, a task that required all his cleverness.

The manner of introduction by the chairman, his name or general position, the appearance of any one of the guests, the lateness or earliness of the hour, events of the day that attract interest, the nature of the entertainment or assemblage—all of these will offer good hooks by which to draw in the story. But let the story be good and thoroughly mastered. Of course the work of adaptation will be much easier if you have several stories in reserve. A story must not be repeated so often that it becomes known as belonging to you, for then a preceding speaker might get a laugh on you by telling it as yours, leaving you bankrupt.

Jones and Smith once rode several miles in a carriage, together, to a town where both were to make addresses. Jones was quite an orator; Smith had a very retentive memory. Jones asked Smith about his speech, but Smith professed not to have fully decided upon his topic, and in turn asked Jones the same question. Jones gave a full outline of his speech, Smith getting him to elaborate it by judicious inquiries as to how he would apply one point and illustrate another. The ride thus passed pleasantly for both parties. Smith was called upon to speak first, and gave with telling effect what he had gathered from Jones, to the delight of everybody, but poor Jones, who listened in utter consternation, and had not strength enough left even to reclaim his stolen property.

If your speech is to be a story it is especially advisable to have a reserve on hand, for stories are easily copied and apt to be long remembered. Care also must be taken that the story is not one with which persons generally are familiar. A gentleman was in the habit of telling a story which has already been quoted, the point of which lies in the phrase "I'm from Boston." Some of his more intimate companions, in self-defense, would exclaim when he proposed a story, "Is it a mile from Boston?"

The definition of the toast itself or of any of the words in the sentiment which is the speaker's topic may be made the occasion for drawing in the illustrative story.

The manner of ending a good story is also worthy of careful study. When an audience is applauding a palpable "hit," it does not seem an appropriate time to stop and take one's seat; but it often is the best course. To do this appears so abrupt that the novice is apt to make a further effort to finish up the subject till he has finished up his audience as well. An attempt to fully discuss a topic, under such circumstances, is not successful once in a hundred times. The best course is to follow an apt story by some proverb, a popular reference, or a witty turn, and then to close. But no abruptness will be disliked by your hearers half so much, as the utterance of a string of commonplaces, after you have once secured their attention. The richness of the dessert should come at the close, not at the beginning, of the oratorical feast.

THE PURPOSE OF AFTER-DINNER SPEAKING

Briefly stated, it is to bring into one focus the thought of an assembly. While the good things of the table may be satisfactory, and conversation free and spontaneous, there is yet need of some expedient for making all thought flow in one channel, and of blending the whole company into a true unity. There is one way, and only one, of doing this—the same that is used to produce unity of action and thought in any assembly, for whatever purpose convened. When the destinies of empires are at stake, when great questions that arise among men are to be solved, the art of speech must be called into play. So after a good dinner has been enjoyed, the same potent agency finds a field, narrower, indeed, but scarcely less operative. And this object—of causing a whole assembly to think the same thoughts and turn their attention to a common topic—is often well attained even when the speeches do not aspire to great excellence or pretension to eloquence.

A commonplace illustration will make our meaning clear. Suppose a great reception, where many rooms are filled with invited guests. There is conversation, but only by groups of two or three persons; refreshments are served; larger groups begin to gather around prominent persons, but there is the same diversity of sentiment and purpose that is to be found in a chance crowd in a public park. The guests are not in one place, with one accord. But now, on some pretext, the power of public speech is evoked; perhaps a toast is offered and responded to, or a more formal address of welcome or congratulation, or anything else suitable to the occasion. The subject and the manner of introduction are not material, so that the living, speaking man is brought face to face with his fellows; at once, instead of confusion and disorder, all is order and harmony. The speaker may hesitate in the delivery of his message, but his very embarrassment will in some instances contribute to harmonize the thought of the assembly even more powerfully than a more pretentious address. But a good and appropriate speech will indelibly fix the thought, and be far more satisfactory.

Where no particular kind of address is indicated by the nature of the assemblage, stories and humor will generally be highly appreciated. A good story has some of the perennial interest that surrounds a romance, and if it is at the same time humorous, an appeal is made to another sentiment, universal in the human breast. If people thrill with interest in unison, or laugh or cry together for a time, or merely give attention to the same thoughts, there will arise a sense of fellowship and sympathy which is not only enjoyable, but is the very purpose for which people are invited to assemblies.

More ordinary after-dinner speeches succeed by the aid of humorous stories than by all other means combined. In a very ingenious book of ready-made speeches the turning point of nearly every one depends upon a pun or other trick of speech. While this is carrying the idea a little too far, still it fairly indicates the importance placed upon sallies of wit or humor as a factor in speech-making. The fellowship that comes from laughing at the same jokes and approving the same sentiments may not be the most intimate or the most enduring, but it is often the only kind possible, and should be prized accordingly.

The chief use of toasts is to call out such speeches, and thus lead the thought of the assembly along pleasant and appropriate channels—all prearranged, yet apparently spontaneous.

A long speech is selfish and unpardonable. It wearies the guests, destroys variety, and crowds others out of the places to which they have been assigned and are entitled. When the speaking is over, the company will have been led to contemplate the same themes, and will have rejoiced, sympathized, and laughed in unison.

SOME A B C DIRECTIONS FOR MAKING SPEECHES, TOASTS, AND RESPONSES

1. Do not be afraid or ashamed to use the best helps you can get. Divest yourself of the idea that all you need is to wait till a toast is proposed and your name called, and then to open your mouth and let the eloquence flow forth. The greatest genius in the world *might* succeed in that way, but would not be likely to venture it. Use a book and study your subject well.

2. Generally, it is not well to memorize word for word either what you have written or obtained from a book, unless it is a pun or a story where the effect depends upon verbal accuracy. But be sure to memorize toasts, sentiments, and titles absolutely. To know the substance of your speech well, with one or two strong points in it, is better than to have a flowery oration weighing down your memory.

3. If you are a novice (and these directions are given to no others), do not aim to make a great speech, but to say a few things modestly and quietly. A short and unassuming speech by a beginner is sure of applause. Eloquence, if you have it in you, will come later through practice and familiarity with your subject.

4. If you can't remember or find a good story, invent one! Perhaps you have scruples as to the latter. But a story is not a lie; if so, what would become of the noble tribe of novel-writers! Mark Twain gives a very humorous account of the way in which he killed his conscience. Probably many speakers who retail good things might make confession in the same direction.

But why is it not as reputable to invent one's own story as to tell the story some one else has invented? Does the second telling improve its morality? Rather give heed to the quality of the story. This, and not its origin, is the really important matter to consider.

5. Success in after-dinner speaking is difficult or easy to attain according to the way you go about it. If you think you must startle, rouse, and electrify your hearers, or, worse still, must instruct them in something *you* think important, but about which they care nothing, your efforts are likely to be attended by a hard and bitter experience. But if, when a prospective speech-occasion looms up, you will reflect upon the sentiment you wish to propose, or will get a friend to do a little planning and suggest the easiest toast or topic, and then attempt to say just a little, you will probably come off with flying colors.

6. When you rise, do not be in a hurry. A little hesitation has a better effect than too much promptness and fluency, and a little stammering or hesitation, it may be added, will have no bad effect. In beginning, your manner can

without disadvantage be altogether lost sight of, and if you have something to say the substance of which is good, and has been carefully prearranged, you will be able to give utterance to it in some form; grammatical mistakes or mispronunciation, where there is no affectation, as well as an occasional repetition, will rarely be noticed.

7. Above all, remember it may be assumed that your hearers are your friends, and are ready to receive kindly what you have to say. This will have a wonderfully steadying effect on your nerves. And if your speech consists only of two or three sentences slowly and deliberately uttered, they will at least applaud its brevity, and give you credit for having filled your place on the programme respectably.

It has been often said that Americans are greatly ahead of the English in general speech-making, but in pleasant after-dinner talking and addresses they are much inferior. Probably this was once true, but if so, it is true no longer. The reason of any former deficiency was simply want of practice, without which no speech-making can be easy and effective. But the importance of this kind of oratory is now recognized, and, with proper efforts to cultivate and master it, Americans are taking the same high rank as in other forms of intellectual effort. Lowell and Depew are acknowledged as peers of any "toast-responder" or "after-dinner orator" the world has ever seen. One of the chief elements of their charm consists in the good stories they relate. Whoever has a natural faculty, be it ever so slight, as a storyteller, will, if he gathers up and appropriates the good things that he meets with, soon realize that he is making rapid progress in this delightful field, and that he gains much more than mere pleasure by his acquisitions.

The best entertainments are not those which merely make a display of wealth and luxury. Quiet, good taste, and social attractions are far better. The English wit, Foote, describes a banquet of the former character. "As to splendor, as far as it went, I admit it: there was a very fine sideboard of plate; and if a man could have swallowed a silversmith's shop, there was enough to satisfy him; but as to all the rest, the mutton was white, the veal was red, the fish was kept too long, the venison not kept long enough; to sum up all, everything was cold except the ice, and everything sour except the vinegar." Excellence in the quality of the viands is not to be disregarded in the choicest company. A celebrated scholar and wit was selecting some of the choicest delicacies on the table, when a rich friend said to him, "What! do philosophers love dainties?" "Why not?" replied the scholar; *do you think all the good things of this world were made only for blockheads?"*

HOLIDAY SPEECHES

FOURTH OF JULY

At a Fourth of July banquet, or celebration, toast may be offered to "The Flag," to "The Day," to "Independence," to "Our Revolutionary Fathers," to "The Nation," to any Great Man of the Past, to "Liberty," to "Free Speech," to "National Greatness," to "Peace," to "Defensive War," to any of the States, to "Washington" or "Lafayette," to "Our Old Ally, France," to any of the "Patriotic Virtues," to "The Army and The Navy," to the "Memory of any of the Battles by Land or Sea." Appropriate sentiments for any of these may easily be devised or may be found in the miscellaneous list in this volume. "The Constitution and the Laws" or something similar should not be omitted.

SOME ITEMS THAT WOULD BE APPROPRIATE IN RESPONDING TO THESE TOASTS.

Their order and character will depend upon the special topic.

Our present prosperity—the greatness and resources of our country as compared with those of the Revolutionary epoch—the slow growth of the colonies—the rapid growth of the States and the addition of new States continually—what was gained by independence—did we do more than simply prevent tyranny—the advantages an independent country possesses over a colony, such as Canada—the perils of independence and the responsibility of power—the romantic early history of the country—the wars that preceded the Revolutionary conflict—the character of the struggle—the slenderness of our resources compared with the mighty power of Britain— our ally, France—what that nation gained and lost by joining in our quarrel— the memories of Washington and Lafayette—the principles at stake in the Revolution—the narrow view our fathers took of the issue at first, and the manner in which they were led first to independence and then to nationality—some phases of the struggle—its critical points—Trenton and Valley Forge—Saratoga and Yorktown—our responsibilities and duties— the questions of that day enumerated and compared with the burning questions of the present day (which we do not enumerate here, but which the speaker may describe or even argue if the nature of his audience, or time at his disposal permits)—the future greatness of the nation—the probability of the acquisition of new territory.

Laughable incidents either from history or illustrations from any source, must not be forgotten, for if the speech be more than a few minutes long they are absolutely indispensable.

OUTLINE OF A SPEECH IN RESPONSE TO THE TOAST "THE DAY WE CELEBRATE"

The Fourth of July has been a great day ever since 1776. Before that year the Fourth of this month came and went like other days. But then a great event happened: an event which made a great difference to the entire world; the boundaries of many countries would be very different to-day if the important event of that day had not transpired. It was a terrible blow to the foes of humanity and even to many weak-kneed friends. The exhortation of one of the signers of the Declaration on that day, "We must all hang together," with the grim but very reasonable rejoinder, "If we do not, we will assuredly hang separately." The bloodshed and suffering which followed and which seem to be the only price at which human liberty and advancement can be procured. We had to deal with our old friends the English very much as the peace-loving Quaker did with the pirate who boarded his ship; taking him by the collar Broad-brim dropped him over the ship's side into the water, saying, "Friend, thee has no business on this ship." We have shown that we own and can navigate the ship of State ourselves, and now we are willing to welcome here not only John Bull but all nations of the world when they have any friendly business with us.

The gunpowder that has been consumed. First, during the Revolutionary war and the second war with England; and then the powder that has been exploded by small and large boys in the hundred and odd Fourths that have followed.

OUTLINE OF A SPREAD-EAGLE SPEECH IN A FOREIGN LAND

We are so far from home that we can't hear the eagle scream or see the lightning in his eye. Only from the almanac do we know that this is the day of all days on which he disports himself. He was a small bird when born, more than a hundred years ago, but has grown lively till his wings reach from ocean to ocean, and it only requires a little faith to see him stretch himself clear over the Western Hemisphere and the adjacent islands. Other birds despised him on the first great Fourth, but these birds of prey, vultures, condors and such like, with crows, as well as the smaller Republican eagles born since, are humble enough to him now. The British lion himself having been so often scratched and clawed by this fowl, has learned to shake his mane and wag his tail rather amiably in our eagle's presence, even if he has to give an occasional growl to keep his hand in. We are proud of this bird, though we are far from home, and to-day send our heartiest good wishes across the sea to the land we love the best.

OUTLINE OF A RESPONSE TO THE TOAST, "OUR COUNTRY"

The field here is very wide. All the history of the country is appropriate, but can only be glanced at, though a good speech might be made by dwelling at length on some romantic incident in its history. The size and richness of the country from the green pine forests of Maine to the golden orange groves of California; or the prophecy of the manifest greatness of coming destiny. Here the old but laughable story can be brought in easily about the raw Irishman who saw a pumpkin for the first time, and was told that it was a mare's egg, and generously given one. He had the misfortune, however, to drop it out of his cart, when it rolled down-hill, struck a stump, burst and frightened a rabbit, which bounded away followed by Pat, shouting: "Shtop my colt; sure and if he is so big and can run so fast now, when just born, what a rousing horse he will be when grown up!"

But our country has more than merely a vast area. She has made advances in science, art, literature, and culture of all kinds, and is destined to play a chief part in the drama of the world's progress.

MEMORIAL DAY

The celebration of this day has become general and has assumed a special and beautiful character. It might have been feared that angry passions engendered by civil strife would predominate, but the very reverse of this is true. Kindness and charity, tender memories of the sacrifices of patriotism, the duty of caring for the living and of avoiding all that might lead again to the sad necessity of war, are the sentiments nearly always inculcated.

The following are a few of the toasts that may be given at celebrations, or banquets, or at the exercises that form a part of the annual decorating of soldiers' graves:

The Martyred Dead—the Regiments locally represented—the Army and Navy—any Dead Soldier especially prominent—the Union Forever—the Whole Country—Victory always for the Right—the Surviving Soldiers and Sailors—Unbroken Peace—the Commander-in-Chief, and other officers locally honored—any special battle whose field is near at hand—the Flag with all its Stars undimmed.

SKETCH OF A SPEECH IN RESPONSE TO THE TOAST, "OUR HONORED DEAD"

Time in its rapid flight tests many things. Thirty years ago the Southern Confederacy, like a dark cloud full of storm and thunderings, covered the Southern heavens. Statesmen planned, preachers prayed, women wept, and armies as brave as ever formed in line fought, for its establishment. Blood flowed freely, and the roar of battle filled the whole land. Many wise men thought it would continue for ages, but lo! it has disappeared. Nothing remains to its adherents but a memory—mournful, pathetic, and bitter.

How different with the Old Flag that we love. It had been tested before, but this was its supreme trial. It had been victorious in several wars. It had sheltered new and expanding States, it had fostered higher forms of civilization, and represented peoples and interests that were complex and varied; but in our Civil War it was assailed as never before. The test was crucial, but nobly was it borne. Men died in ranks as the forest goes down before the cyclone. What sharp agony in death, and what long-continued suffering and bereavement this implies. But the result was decisive—a strengthening of the power and grandeur of the nation that sometimes seems to be only too great and unquestioned.

We have no wish by any word of ours to revive bitter feeling or stir up strife. This hallowed day has been from the first a peacemaker. Men, standing with uncovered heads in the presence of the dead, do not care to utter words of reproach for the irrevocable past. We, wearing the blue, can say to the scarred veteran wearers of the gray: "You fought well for the lost cause. But the case was fairly tried in the awful court of war. It took four years for the jury to agree, but the verdict has been given—a verdict against your cause—and there is no higher court and no appeal. There is no resurrection for the dead Confederacy; but we can offer you something better—an equal part in the life and destiny of the most glorious nation time has yet produced." And on their side the gray can reply, in the words of Colonel Grady, the eloquent orator of the South, in his speech at Atlanta: "We can now see that in this conflict loss was gain, and defeat real and substantial victory; that everything we hoped for and fought for, in the new government we sought to establish, is given to us in greater measure in the old government our fathers founded."

We do not meet on these Memorial Days to weep for the dead, as we did while wounds were yet fresh. Time has healed the scars of war, and we can calmly contemplate the great lesson of patriotic devotion, and rejoice that the nation to which we belong produced men noble enough to die for that which they valued so much. Neither do I care to say anything of human slavery, the institution that died and was buried with the Confederacy. I had enough to say about it while it was living. Let the dead past bury its dead.

But we are here to foster patriotism, in view of the most tremendous sacrifice ever willingly made by a people on the altar of nationality. That the sacrifices of the Civil War deserve this rank will appear from the fact that they were made—in the main—by volunteers. We were not fighting directly to defend our altars and our fires; we were not driven to arms to repel an invading foe; we were not hurried to the field by king or noble; but in the first flush of manhood we offered ourselves to preserve unimpaired the unity, the purity, the glory of our nation. So far as I have turned over the leaves of the volume of time, I have found nothing in all the past like this. Therefore, standing before the highest manifestation of earthly patriotism, viewing it crowned in all the glory of self-sacrifice, by a faithfulness which was literally in the case of hundreds of thousands "unto death," we ask: "What is there that justifies a nation in exacting or accepting (when freely offered) such tribute of the life-blood of its people?"

The two things of inestimable value which our government furnishes and which we ought to preserve even with life itself, if the sacrifice is needed, are liberty and law, or rather liberty *in* law. The old world gave law, without which human society cannot exist. But it was accompanied with terrible suffering— as when "order reigned in Warsaw." Such law came from masters, and made the mass of the people slaves. We have an equal perfection of law, order, subordination, but it rises side by side with liberty The people govern themselves—not in one form of government alone but in affairs national, State, county, down to the smallest school district and a thousand voluntary societies. In each the methods by which the people's will may be made supreme in designated affairs are clearly defined, so that the whole of united human effort is brought under the dominion of law, even such things as general education, and yet each affair is in the hands of the people directly concerned. For thousands of years the principles of our complex and wonderful system of co-ordinated government have been growing up till they have reached their fullest perfection on our soil, and we breathe their beneficence as we breathe the air of heaven. Men are willing to die by the tens of thousands that this liberty under law may not perish from the world.

... Comrades and Citizens:—We move forward to new issues and new responsibilities. Grave dangers are now upon us. God grant that they may not need to be met and settled in the rude shock of war. The time for wisdom, for clear-sighted patriotism is—*now*. Labor and capital, the foundations of law and order; the complex civilization of a nation which now talks by lightning, and is hurled by steam over plains and mountains, and which, doubtless, will soon fly through the air—all these are to be settled by the men now on the stage of action. We cannot do better than to tell you, to settle them in the spirit of the men whose great sacrifices we to-day commemorate.

OUTLINE OF A SPEECH BY CHAUNCEY M. DEPEW, ON A DECORATION [MEMORIAL] DAY.

This is one of the most interesting of national celebrations, appealing not to pride, but to tender personal memories. But we must not give ourselves up wholly to sadness or mourning. The story of issues and results must be told.

Why did our heroes die? On account of the cancer of slavery and the resulting doctrine of State Rights. Nationality and liberty, the opposite view. The former was the party of action, and, therefore, though in a minority, it was bolder and more determined. But the shell of materialism dropped from the North, and it was aroused with electric energy when Sumter was fired on; there was no passion, only such fervid resolve to preserve our nation as the world never before saw. The struggle over, there were no State trials, no prisons nor scaffolds, and the Republic, though bleeding at every pore, said to the conquered enemy, "Come and share fully with us all the blessings of our preserved institutions," and thus won a second victory greater than the first.

The wonderful intelligence of the volunteer—story of Napoleon's soldier—"Dead on the field of honor."

The Grand Army of the elect—the heroes of history, some of whom are enumerated—the actual value to a nation of such heroism. To-day all that belongs to the strife is forgiven, but its lessons are too noble and precious ever to be forgotten. We can all, North and South, read with enthusiasm the story of each varied and romantic campaign.

The Confederate women first began decorating the graves of their dead with flowers, and did not pass by the Union graves near their late foes. This touched the heart of the nation as nothing else could have done, and enmity melted away, and the observance of the day has become universal.

The two great national heroes—Washington, with his wise, foresighted "Farewell Address;" Lincoln, with his gentle spirit, his martyr death, and his tender words, "With malice towards none, with charity for all." Washington the Founder, Lincoln the Preserver.

WASHINGTON'S BIRTHDAY

APPROPRIATE TOASTS

To Washington—to The Great Men of Revolutionary Times—to The Great Man who could not do what many modern Politicians can do—*tell a lie*—to The Childless Father of Eighty Millions of people—to The American Model Statesman—to The Greatest of Good Men and the Best of Great Men.

THOUGHTS FOR A SPEECH IN RESPONSE TO THE TOAST "WASHINGTON: GREAT AS A SOLDIER, GREATER AS A STATESMAN, GREATEST AS A PURE PATRIOT"

Indian, French, and English enemies. He had to make the armies with which he conquered. He was always a safe commander, but full of enterprise also—his character made the Union of the States and the Constitution possible. His character the best inheritance of the American people. Other men as great, possibly in some instances greater in a single field—his greatness shown in the wide union of the noblest kinds of greatness, all in harmony.

HUMOROUS RESPONSE BY BENJAMIN F. BUTLER TO THE TOAST, "OUR FOREFATHERS"

"While venerating their lofty patriotism, may we emulate them in their republican simplicity of manners." He declared that a great deal had been said at one time and another about the democratic simplicity of our forefathers. Suppose that the gentlemen of the present day should go back to some of the customs of the forefathers. Suppose a man should go to a ball nowadays in the costume in which Thomas Jefferson, "that great apostle of democratic simplicity," once appeared in Philadelphia. What a sensation he would create with his modest (?) costume of velvet and lace, with knee-breeches, silk stockings, silver shoe-buckles, and powdered wig. "Even the great father of his country had a little style about him," said the speaker. "It was a known fact that he never went to Congress when he was President unless he went in a coach and six, with a little cupid on the box bearing a wreath of flowers. The coach must be yellow and the horses white, and then the President's secretary usually followed in a coach drawn by four horses. When Washington ascended the steps to enter the doors, he always stopped for a moment and turned slowly around to allow an admiring people to see the father of their country. Oh! our forefathers were saturated with modesty and simplicity. The people of the present day have retrograded greatly from the simplicity of their Revolutionary ancestors. I can remember when it was impossible, years before the war, to hold a night session of Congress. It was impossible because the members of Congress attended dinners, and lingered over their wine. They attended dinners very like the one we have just enjoyed, and yet there is not a man in this company who is unfitted to attend to any public or private duties that might demand his attention. Yes, it is true that we have departed from the old customs, but we have advanced and not retrograded. The world has changed, but it has changed for the better. It is growing better every day, and don't let anybody forget it."

CHRISTMAS
APPROPRIATE TOASTS

The Day of Good-will—to The Cold Weather without and the Warm Hearts within—to The Christmas Tree, which grows in a Night and is plucked in the Morning by the gladdest of fingers—to The Day in which Religion gives sweetness to Social Life—Christmas Gifts; may they bless the Giver not less than the Receiver—to The Oldest of our Festivals, which grows mellower and sweeter with the passage of the centuries—to St. Nicholas [or Santa Claus], the only saint Protestants worship—to A Merry Day that leaves no heart-ache—to A Good Christmas, may sleighing, gifts, and feasting crowd out all gambling and drunkenness.

SPEECH-THOUGHTS

The good cheer enjoyed on this merriest day of the year. How the little people look forward to it. It comes to the older ones as a joy, and yet tender and sad with the memories of other Christmases. The religious and the secular elements of the day. The countries where it is most observed. The long contest between the two days, Thanksgiving and Christmas. The compromise that Massachusetts and Virginia, New England and the South, have unanimously agreed upon; namely, to keep both days.

SELECTED OUTLINE OP AN EFFECTIVE LITTLE CHRISTMAS SPEECH

The speaker assumes that the observance of the day is becoming obsolete, and that there are persons who wish it to die out. The assumption, though rather strained, affords the opportunity to demolish this man of straw. "All other kings may go, but no one can spare King Christmas, or St. Nicholas, his prime minister. School-rooms and nurseries would rebel. And plum pudding is too strongly entrenched in Church and State to be dislodged. Washington Irving, with his *Sketch Book*, would protest. Best argument of all is the worth of the Christmas entertainments. Here's to the Festival of Festivals, and long may its honors be done by such hosts as entertain us to-day."

THANKSGIVING

Coming at the beginning of the farmer's rest, when the harvest is all gathered, this is a very joyous festival, and more than any other abounds in family reunions. Any toast therefore is appropriate which tells of the harvest, of fertility, of the closing year, of the family pride and traditions, of pleasure to young and old. At dinner, turkey and mince or pumpkin pie will of course be served, and these national favorites must not be forgotten by the toastmaker.

This day, too, has an official and governmental flavor given to it by the State and national proclamations which fix the date and invite its observance. Usually, these enumerate the blessings enjoyed by the whole country during the year, and suggest topics peculiarly fitting for toasts. It is perhaps not too much to say that Thanksgiving is distinctly *the* American Festival, and should be honored accordingly.

TOASTS

To The Inventor of Pumpkin Pie—to Peace with all Nations—to The Rulers of our Country—to The Farmer—to Full Stomachs and Merry Hearts—to their Excellencies, the President and the Governor; may we obey all their commands as willingly as when they tell us to feast—Abounding Plenty; may we always remember the Source from which our benefits come—Our two National Fowls, the American Eagle and the Thanksgiving Turkey; may the one give us peace for all our States and the other a piece for all our plates— The Turkey and the Eagle; we love to have the one soar high, but wish the other to roost low—The Great American Birds; may we have them where we love them best, the Turkeys on our tables and the Eagles in our pockets.

THOUGHTS FOR A THANKSGIVING SPEECH

The manner in which the day was first instituted. The sore struggles and the small beginnings of that day compared with the greatness and abounding prosperity of the present. The warfare between Christmas and Thanksgiving, the one being thought the badge of popery and prelacy. The Battle of the Pies, pumpkin and mince, terminating in a treaty of peace and alliance; and now we can enjoy the nightmare by feasting on both combined! The national blessings of the year; the poorest have more now than kings and emperors had five hundred years ago. Exemption from wars. Internal peace. Willingness and habit of settling every domestic dispute by the ballot, and not the bullet. The increasing tendency to arbitrate between nations, thus avoiding the horrors of war. The beneficence of our government and the ease with which its operations rest upon our shoulders. The wonderful progress of science and invention, and the manner in which these have added to the comfort of all the people.

SELECTED OUTLINE FOE A THANKSGIVING SPEECH

Why we ought to be grateful to the old Puritans, with all their faults. Their unsuccessful warfare on plum pudding, which, like truth, "crushed to earth," rose again. Their discovery and enshrining of Turkey. On this day the Nation gathers as a family at the Thanksgiving board, and from all parts of the world the wanderers come home to the family feast. The duty of Happiness, joined to gratitude, is emphasized this day. The closing toast, "The Federal Eagle and the Festal Turkey; may we always have peace under the wings of the one, and be able to obtain a piece from the breast of the other."

PRESENTATION ADDRESSES

Giving a present is a kind and graceful act, and should be accompanied by a simple, short, and unaffected speech. "Take this" would have the merit of brevity, but would fail in conveying any information as to *who* gave, why they gave *to the recipient*, and why *that* present was selected rather than another, and why *the speaker* was chosen to make the presentation. All of these items form a part of nearly every presentation address, whilst some of them belong to all.

The novice will find much help in preparing his proposed speech by selecting a few items that are generally appropriate; afterward he can include anything which his own genius or wishes may suggest.

He may say that an abler speaker might have been selected for the pleasant duty, but not one who could enter into it more heartily or with more good wishes. He can refer to any circumstance which, if told briefly, will show why he has been selected, notwithstanding his reluctance or sense of unworthiness; or why he is pleased that the selection has fallen upon him. Such reference is usually effective.

Then the nature of the gift may be described. Here is an easy field for a little pleasantry. If a watch, it can be said, "Your friends are growing a little suspicious of you, and, after due deliberation, they have determined to a place *a watch* upon you." If a cane is the article in hand, then the painful duty of administering punishment for offenses by *caning* is in order. A ring will afford an opportunity for many verbal plays. The ring of friends about the recipient, the true ring of a bell, or of an uncracked vase, a political ring—any of these can be made to lead up to the little hoop of gold. The fineness of the material, its sterling and unvarying value, the inscription on it, any specialty in its form—all these will be found rich in suggestion. Silverware of any kind may also be considered as to the form of the article, the use to which it is to be put, and the purity of the metal. Hardly any article can be thought of which will not allow some pleasant puns or *bon mots*. If a book is given, we bring the person "to book," and the book to him. Job wished that his enemy might write a book; we, more charitable, wish our friend to read a book, and now offer him a good one for the purpose. The author or the title will, if closely examined, yield some matter for play on words.

The army presents of sword or banner, while usually more serious, do not forbid the same kind of badinage.

But this should form only a small portion of the speech, and consist merely of two or three well-studied sentences, to be uttered slowly, so that their double meaning may have time to sink in, and appear also as if they were just thought of. A good anecdote should be introduced at this point. It must be short, tinged with humor, and, if it succeeds in arousing the attention of the hearers, it will be of great value. If it is very appropriate or highly illustrative, these qualities will compensate for humor. Indeed, a felicitous anecdote will make the whole speech a success, if the speech is not continued too long afterward. Better suffer the extreme penalty of reading every anecdote in this volume, and of searching for hours in other fields, than fail to get the right one; but if unsuccessful invent one for the occasion!

The good qualities of the recipient must not be overlooked, especially those in recognition of which the present is given. If anything in the nature of the present itself can be made symbolic of these assumed good or great qualities, it will be a happy circumstance. And while flattery should not be excessive or too palpable, it is seldom indeed that a large dose of "pleasant things" will not be well received by all parties on such an occasion.

The expression of kindly feeling and good wishes always affords a favorable opportunity for closing. Perhaps, however, a more striking conclusion can be made by taking advantage of the very moment when the present is handed over to the recipient, accompanying this act with a hearty wish for its long retention and its happy use in the manner its nature indicates. Wishing a ring to be worn as a memento of friendship, a watch to mark the passage of happy hours, a cane not to be needed for support, but only as a treasured ornament, a sword to be worn with honor and only to be unsheathed at the call of duty or of patriotism, etc.

The reception of a gift is more easy than the presentation, but is at the same time more embarrassing. The reception is easier, because the essential part of the response is to say "Thank you," which are very easy words to utter if the givers are real friends and the present is an appropriate one. It is more embarrassing because it is always harder to receive a favor gratefully than to give one. If the gift is a surprise, there is no harm in saying so, though if it is not a surprise, it is not advisable to tell an untruth about it. The recipient may say he is embarrassed, and his embarrassment—whether real or feigned— will create sympathy for him. Besides, he can ask for indulgence with more grace than the preceding speaker, as he is supposed to be taken by surprise. He may be so overcome with emotion as to break down altogether, and yet he will be loudly applauded.

A still stronger reason for this disparity is that the speaker representing the givers has been selected, probably out of a large company, to make his speech, and is thus expected to do it well; but the receiver occupies *his* position for a reason that has no connection whatever with his speech-making powers. If he succeeds in expressing his gratitude and goodwill to those who have been so generous he will have served the essential purpose of his speech; but if, in addition, he can gather up the points made in the presentation speech, assenting to its general principles, accepting the humorous charges for which he is to be watched, caned, stoned (when a diamond or other stone is given), or put to the sword, and gently deprecates the serious flattery offered, he will be regarded as doing exceedingly well. One phrase he will not be likely to omit, unless "he loses his head" altogether—"When I look upon this, I will always remember the feelings of this hour, the kind words uttered, the appreciation shown." This word "appreciation." with the reiteration of thanks, will make a very fitting conclusion.

ADDRESSES OF WELCOME

In our country the number of voluntary associations that visit similar associations, or meet at special times and places is very large. Often such associations are furnished with free board and lodging by the people of the place where the assemblage occurs. Facilities for assemblage and enjoyment are offered and other privileges tendered that are highly appreciated. Religious bodies, church and philanthropic societies, military and fire companies, athletic and social clubs, various orders and educational societies, political bodies, these form only a small proportion of the endless number of organizations convening and gathering at different centres, gatherings which serve to keep all parts of our country in close touch.

It is needless to furnish model speeches for each of these, for the same general line of remark is adapted to all. The changes of illustration demanded by the character of the association to be welcomed, and for which responses are to be made, will be readily understood, and a little study of the name and character of the place of meeting will make the necessary local allusions quite easy. The welcome and response for a fire company, or a baseball club, will not differ much from that for a Christian Endeavor Society. A few general hints and a little investigation by the novice will put him on the right track in either case.

ADDRESS OF WELCOME

A clear statement about those who extend the welcome and of those who are to be welcomed is appropriate. This may be expanded advantageously by giving a few of the characteristics of each, greater latitude being allowed in complimenting those who are welcomed than those who entertain. It is bad taste to spend more time in telling our guests how good and great we are than in expressing the exalted opinion we have of them for their noble work, their great fame, or their high purpose; or in declaring the pleasure we feel and the honor we have in entertaining them. The warmth of the welcome extended should be expressed in the fullest manner, and as this is the central purpose of the whole address, it will bear *one repetition*. A good illustrative story, brief but pointed, may be worked in somewhere, perhaps in connection with a modest depreciation of our own fitness or ability adequately to express the strong feelings of those we represent, though if one can be found having a connection with the visitors themselves, it will be still better. What we wish our visitors to do while with us may also be appropriately referred to. If there are places of interest for them to visit, work for them to do, or special entertainments provided,—here is additional matter for remark. All these items may be run through in a few minutes, and then the address should close. The most bungling and formal welcome, if short, will be enjoyed more and be more applauded than the most graceful and eloquent one unduly prolonged. Should however, in spite of this warning, more "filling in" be desired of an appropriate character, it may be found almost without limit in setting forth the claim of the cause which both the visitors and the entertainers represent—athletic sports, religion, benevolence, education, or what not.

ADDRESS IN RESPONSE

This may be still more brief than the address of welcome. To say that the reception is hearty, that it gives pleasure and is gratefully received and appreciated, is all that is essential. An invitation to return the visit should not be forgotten, if circumstances are such that it can be appropriately made. Then the speaker has an opportunity to review any portion of the preceding speech and express his indorsement of any of the assertions made. He should not dissent from them, unless this dissent can be made the means of a little adroit flattery by placing a higher estimate upon the entertainers and their services than their own speaker has done, or by modestly disclaiming some of the praise that has been given. The novice must avoid being carried too far by this fascinating review, both as to the quantity and the quality of the disagreement.

A closing sentence may be, "Allow me once more, most heartily, to thank you for this generous welcome to—your homes—your headquarters—to the hospitalities of your city," as the case may be.

WEDDING AND OTHER ANNIVERSARIES

Another wide field for the oratory of entertainment is to be found in the various celebrations that mark the passage of specific or notable portions of time—centennial, semi-centennial, and quadrennial; likewise weddings, annual, tin, paper, crystal, silver, and golden. The speeches for these differ widely in character. They may take the form of congratulatory addresses, of toasts and responses, or more formal addresses. All dedications come in the same category. Generally the shorter intervals call for light and humorous speeches, while the longer ones demand something more grave and thoughtful.

The following speech and response for a wooden (fifth) wedding anniversary is taken from a volume of ready made speeches. It is a fine example of that wit and play upon words which is never more suitable or more highly appreciated than on such an occasion.

SPEECH FOR A WOODEN WEDDING

If it is a good maxim not to halloo till you are out of the woods, our kind host and hostess must be very quiet this evening, for it seems to me that they are in the thick of it. If their friends had been about to burn them alive instead of to wish them joy on their fifth wedding-day, they could scarcely have brought a greater quantity of combustible material to the sacrifice. What shall we say to them on this ligneous occasion? Of course, we must congratulate them on their willingness to renew their matrimonial vows after five years of double-blessedness. In this age of divorce it is something worthy of note, that a pair who have been one and inseparable for even so short a period as the twentieth part of a century, should stand up proudly before the world and propose to strengthen the original compact with a new one. They look as happy and contented as if they had never heard of Chicago, or seen those tempting little advertisements in the newspapers that propose to separate man and wife with immediate dispatch for a reasonable consideration. Instead of going to court to cut the nuptial bond in twain, it appears that they have been *courting* for five years with the view of being remarried this evening. Vaccination, it is said, wears out in seven years, but matrimony, we see, in this instance, at least, takes a stronger hold of the parties inoculated as time rolls on; and although in this case they are willing to go through the operation again, it is not for the sake of making assurance doubly sure, but in order to enjoy marriage as a luxury. With this happy specimen of a wooden wedding before them our young unmarried friends will see that they can go into the *joinery* business with but little risk of getting into the wrong box. In fact, it is because connubial bliss beats every other species of felicity all hollow that we have met this evening to requite it with hollow-ware. In the name of all their friends I affectionately congratulate the doubly-married pair on their past happiness and future prospects, and hope they may live to celebrate their fiftieth wedding day and receive a *golden* reward.

BRIDEGROOM IN REPLY

"For self and partner"—as men associated in business sometimes conclude their letters—I offer to you and all our friends who have obliged us with their presence, the thanks of the firm which renews its articles of partnership this evening. We welcome you heartily to our home, well knowing that your kind wishes are not like—your useful and elegant tokens of remembrance—*hollow-ware*. When Birnam Wood came to Dunsinane, Macbeth was conquered, and it seems to me that you have come almost as well provided with timber as Macduff and Malcolm were. Your articles, however, although of wood, are not of the Burn 'em kind, and I am not such a Dunce inane as to decline accepting them. Indeed, my wife, who, notwithstanding her matrimonial vows, has a *single eye*—to housekeeping—would not permit me to refuse them were I so inclined. She knows their value better than I do, and with the assistance of her kitchen cabinet will, I have no doubt, employ them usefully.

The speech closes with thanks and good wishes in return.

TOASTS

A toast may be given either with or without sentiment attached, and in either case a response equally fitting; but in the former the subject is narrowed and defined by the nature of the sentiment. Yet the speaker need not hold himself closely to the sentiment, which is often made rather a point of departure even by the ablest speakers. Indeed, the latitude accorded to after-dinner speeches is very great, and a sentiment which gives unity and direction to the speech made in response to it is, on that account, of great value.

To illustrate these points we will take the toast "Our Flag." A speech in response would be practically unlimited in scope of treatment. Anything patriotic, historical or sentimental, which brings in some reference to the banner, would be appropriate. But let this sentiment be added: "May the justness and benevolence which it represents ever charm the heart, as its beauty charms the eye," and the outline of a speech is already indicated. Has our nation always been just and kind? Where and how have these qualities been most strikingly manifested? Why have we seemed sometimes to come short of them, and how should such injustice or harsh dealing be remedied, with as much rhetorical admixture of the waving folds and the glittering stars as the speaker sees fit to employ.

From these considerations may be deduced the rule that when the proposer of a toast wishes to leave the respondent the freedom of the whole subject he will give the toast alone, or accompanied by a motto of the most non-committal character. But if he wishes to draw him out in a particular direction he will put the real theme in the sentiment that follows the toast.

SENTIMENTS SUGGESTED BY A TOAST

Years ago a speaker provoked a controversy (maliciously and with no good excuse) which scarcely came short of blows, by proposing as a toast the name of a general of high rank, but who was unfortunate in arms. He was a candidate for office. Added to the toast was the sentiment, "May his political equal his military victories." This was in bad taste, indeed, but it shows the use that can be made of the sentiment, when added to a toast, in fixing attention in a certain direction.

The number of sentiments suggested by the common and standard toasts is unlimited. Take the toast "Home," as an example.

Home: The golden setting in which the brightest jewel is "Mother."

Home: A world of strife shut out, and a world of love shut in.

Home: The blossoms of which heaven is the fruit.

Home: The only spot on earth where the fault and failings of fallen humanity are hidden under a mantle of charity.

Home: An abode wherein the inmate, the superior being called man, can pay back at night, with fifty per cent. interest, every annoyance that he has met with in business during the day.

Home: The place where the great are sometimes small, and the small often great.

Home: The father's kingdom; the child's paradise; the mother's world.

Home: The jewel casket containing the most precious of all jewels—domestic happiness.

Home: The place where you are treated best and grumble most.

Home: It is the central telegraph office of human love, into which run innumerable wires of affection, many of which, though extending thousands of miles, are never disconnected from the one great terminus.

Home: The centre of our affections, around which our hearts' best wishes twine.

Home: A little sheltered hollow scooped out of the windy hill of the world.

Home: A place where our stomachs get three good meals daily and our hearts a thousand.

MISCELLANEOUS TOASTS

These might be multiplied indefinitely, but a sufficient number are given to serve as hints to the person who is able to make his own toasts, yet seeks a little aid to lift him out of the common rut.

Marriage: The happy estate which resembles a pair of shears; so joined that they cannot be separated; often moving in opposite directions, yet always punishing any one who comes between them.

Marriage: The gate through which the happy lover leaves his enchanted ground and returns from paradise to earth.

Woman: The fairest work of the great Author; the edition is large, and no man should be without a copy.

Woman: She needs no eulogy; she speaks for herself.

Woman: The bitter half of man. (A sour bachelor's toast.)

Wedlock: May the single all be married and all the married be happy. Love to one, friendship to many, and good-will to all.

The Lady we love and the Friend we trust.

May we have the unspeakable good Fortune to win a true heart, and the Merit to keep it.

Friendship: May its bark never founder on the rocks of deception.

Friendship: May its lamp ever be supplied by the oil of truth and fidelity.

Unselfish Friendship: May we ever be able to serve a friend, and noble enough to conceal it.

Firm Friendship: May differences of opinion only cement it.

May we have more and more Friends and Need them less and less.

May our Friend in sorrow never be a Sorrowing friend.

Active Friendship: May the hinges of friendship never grow rusty.

To our Friends: Whether absent on land or sea.

Our Friends: May the present have no burdens for them and futurity no terrors.

Our Friends: May we always have them and always know their value.

Friends: May we be richer in their love than in wealth, and yet money be plenty.

A Friend: May we never want one to cheer us, or a home to welcome him.

Good Judgment: May opinions never float in the sea of ignorance.

Careful Kindness: May we never crack a joke or break a reputation.

Enduring Prudence: May the pleasures of youth never bring us pain in old age.

Deliverance in Trouble: May the sunshine of hope dispel the clouds of calamity.

Successful Suit: May we court and win all the Daughters of Fortune except the eldest—Miss Fortune.

Here's a Health to Detail, Retail, and Curtail—indeed, all the tails but tell-tales.

The Coming Millennium: When great men are honest and honest men are great.

Our Merchant: May he have good trade, well paid. May the Devil cut the toes of all our foes, That we may know them by their limping.

May we Live to learn well and Learn to live well.

A Placid Life: May we never murmur without cause, and never have cause to murmur.

May we never lose our Bait when we Fish for compliments.

A Better Distribution of Money: May Avarice lose his purse and Benevolence find it.

May Care be a stranger and Serenity a familiar friend to every honest heart.

May Fortune recover her eyesight and be able to distribute her gifts more wisely and equally.

May Bad Example never attract youthful minds.

May Poverty never come to us without rich compensations and hope of a speedy departure.

Our Flag: The beautiful banner that represents the precious *mettle* of America.

American Eagle, The: The liberty bird that permits no liberties.

American Eagle, The: May she build her nest in every rock peak of this continent.

American Valor: May no war require it, but may it be always ready for every foe.

American People, The: May they live in peace and grow strong in the practice of every virtue.

Our Native Land: May it ever be worthy of our heartiest love, and continue to draw it forth without stint.

(A spread-eagle toast.) The Boundaries of Our Country: East, by the Rising Sun; north, by the North Pole; west, by all Creation; and south, by the Day of Judgment.

Our Lakes and Rivers: Navigable waters that unite all the States and render the very thought of their separation absurd.

Our Sons and Daughters: May they be honest as brave and modest as fair.

America and the World: May our nation ever enjoy the blessings of the widest liberty, and be ever ready to promote the liberties of mankind.

Discontented Citizens: May they speedily leave their country for their country's good.

America:

"Our hearts, our hopes are all with thee,

  Our hearts, our hopes, our prayers, our tears,

  Our faith, triumphant o'er our fears,

 Are all with thee, are all with thee."

The Patriot:

 "Breathes there a man with soul so dead,

 Who never to himself hath said,

  This is my own, my native land;

 Whose heart hath ne'er within him burned,

 As home his footsteps he hath turned

  From wandering on a foreign strand?"

Our Country: Whether bounded by Canada or Mexico, or however otherwise bounded and described; be the measurement more or less, still Our Country; to be cherished in our hearts and defended by our lives.

Our Country: In our intercourse with foreign nations may she always be in the right; and if not, may we ever be true patriots enough to get her into the right at any cost.

Our Country: May we render due reverence and love to the common mother of us all.

The Ship of State:

 "Nail to the mast her holy flag;

  Set every threadbare sail;

 And give her to the God of Storms,

  The lightning and the gale."

Columbia: My country, with all thy faults, I love thee still.

Webster's Motto: Liberty and Union, now and forever, one and inseparable.

True Patriotism: May every American be a good citizen in peace, a valiant soldier in war.

Our Country: May our love of country be without bounds and without a shadow of fear.

Our Statesmen: May they care less for party and for personal ambition than for the nation's welfare.

Failure to Treason: May he who would destroy his country for a mess of pottage never get the pottage!

The Penalty of Treason: May he who would uproot the tree of Liberty be the first one crushed by its fall.

The Nation: May it know no North, no South, no East, no West, but only one broad, beautiful, glorious land.

America:

Dear Country, our thoughts are more constant to thee,

Than the steel to the star and the stream to the sea.

Our Revolutionary Fathers: May their sons never disgrace their parentage.

Our Town: The best in the land; let him that don't like it leave it.

The Tree of Liberty: May every American citizen help cultivate it and eat freely of its fruit.

The Emigrant: May the man that doesn't love his native country speedily hie him to one that he can love.

The American Eagle: It is not healthful to try to deposit salt on his venerable tail.

California: The land of golden rocks and golden fruits.

Ohio: The second Mother of Presidents.

Vermont: A State of rocks, but producing men, women, maple sugar, and horses.

"The first are strong, the last are fleet,

The second and third are exceedingly sweet,

And all are uncommonly hard to beat."

Texas: The biggest of States, and one of the very best.

New York: Unrivalled if numbers in city and State be the test.

Our Navy: May it always be as anxious to preserve peace as to uphold the honor of the flag in war.

Our Army: May it ever be very small in peace, but grow to mighty dimensions and mightier achievement in war.

Our Country: May the form of liberty never be used to subvert the principles of true freedom.

Our Voters: May they always have a standard to try their rulers by, and be quick to punish or reward justly.

Fortune: A divinity to fools, a helper to wise men.

The Present: Anticipation may be very agreeable but participation is more practical.

The Present Opportunity: We may lay in a stock of pleasures for use in memory, but they must be kept carefully to prevent mouldering.

Philosophy: It may conquer past or present pain but toothache, while it lasts, laughs at philosophy.

Our Noble Selves: Why not toast ourselves and praise ourselves since we have the best means of knowing all the good in ourselves?

Charity: A link from the chain of gold that angels forge.

Our Harvests: May the sunshine of plenty dispel the clouds of care.

Virtue: May we have the wit to discover what is true and the fortitude to practice what is good.

Our Firesides: Our heads may not be sharpened at colleges, but our hearts are graduates of the hearths.

The True Medium: Give us good form, but not formality.

The Excesses of Youth: They are heavy drafts upon old age, payable with compound interest about thirty years from date.

The Best of Good Feeling: May we never feel want nor want feeling.

Our Incomes: May we have a head to earn and hearts to spend.

Forbearance: May we have keen wit, but never make a sword of our tongues to wound the reputation of others.

Wit: A cheap and nasty commodity when uttered at the expense of modesty and courtesy.

Cheerfulness and Fortitude: May we never give way to melancholy, but always be merry at the right places.

Generosity: May we all be as charitable and indulgent as the Khan of Tartary, who, when he has dined on milk and horseflesh, makes proclamation that all the kings and emperors of earth have now his gracious permission to dine.

Economy: The daughter of Prudence, the sister of Temperance, and the parent of Independence.

Fidelity and Forgiveness: May our injuries be written in sand and our gratitude for benefits in rock.

A Good Memory: May it always be used as a storehouse and never as a lumber-room.

A Health to Our Dearest: May their purses always be heavy and their hearts always be light.

The Noblest Qualities: Charity without ostentation and religion without bigotry.

Discernment of Character: May Flattery never be permitted to sit in the parlor while Plain and Kindly Dealing is kicked out into the woodshed.

False Friends: May we never have friends who, like shadows, keep close to us in the sunshine only to desert us in a cloudy day or in the night.

A Competence: May we never want bread to make a toast or a good cook to prepare it.

The Man we Love: He who thinks most good and speaks least ill of his neighbors.

Human Nature as the Best Study: He who is learned in books alone may know how some things ought to be, but he who reads men learns how things are.

Metaphysics the Noblest of the Sciences: "When a mon wha' kens naething aboot ony subject, takes a subject that nae mon kens onything aboot and explains it to anither mon still more ignorant—that's Metaphysics."

The Deeds of Men: The best interpreters of their motives.

Love and Affection: The necessary basis for a happy life.

Charity: A mantle of heavenly weaving used to cover the faults of our neighbors.

Charitable Allowances: May our eyes be no keener when we look upon the faults of others than when we survey our own.

Cheerful Courage: "May this be our maxim whene'er we are twirled, A fig for the cares of this whirl-a-gig world."

A Golden Maxim: To err is human, to forgive divine.

Prudence in Speech: The imprudent man reflects upon what he has said, the wise man upon what he is going to say.

Thought and Speech: It is much safer to always think what we say than always to say what we think.

Everybody: May no one now feel that he has been omitted.

Fame: The great undertaker who pays little attention to the living but makes no end of parade over the dead.

The Chatterbox: May he give us a few brilliant flashes of silence.

Discretion in Speech: May we always remember the manner, the place, and the time.

A Happy Future: May the best day we have seen be worse than the worst that is to come.

HUMOROUS TOASTS.

To a Fat Friend: May your shadow never grow less.

May every Hair of your head be as a shining Candle to light you to glory.

Long Life to our Friends: May the chicken never be hatched that will scratch on their graves.

Confusion to the Early Bird: May it and the worm both be picked up.

The Nimble Penny: May it soon grow into a dime and then swell into a dollar.

To a Sovereign: not the kind that sits on a throne, but the one that lies in our pocket.

Our Land: May we live happy in it and never be sent out of it for our country's good.

Three Great Commanders: May we always be under the orders of General Peace, General Plenty, and General Prosperity.

The Three Best Doctors: May Doctor Quiet, Doctor Diet, and Doctor Good Conscience ever keep us well.

The Health of that wise and good Man who kept a Dog and yet did his own barking!

Here's to the health of ——: The old bird that was not caught with chaff.

The Health of those we Love the beet; Our noble selves.

MISCELLANEOUS ADDRESSES

Every year new occasions arise that point to a new order of celebrations. Until recently there were no centennial celebrations. Once inaugurated these suggested semi-centennial and quarter-century ones, and as the country advanced in years there came the bi-centennial and ter-centennial. And the attention of the civilized globe was called to our fourth-centennial by the unrivalled and wonderful display at the World's Exhibition in Chicago.

In this chapter are given outlines of a miscellaneous character, some original and some selected.

OUTLINE OF CHAUNCEY M. DEPEW'S ADDRESS AT THE CENTENNIAL OF CAPTURE OF ANDRÉ

This is a good model for the semi-centennial or centennial of any noted event.

Being in the open air the speaker referred to the grand scenery, almost the same as one hundred years before.

Effect on the nation's heart of such Revolutionary commemorations.

Small events influence the currents of history. Thermopylæ and its 300; *the three plain farmers who preserved American liberty.*

The orator then sketched compactly but vividly the critical situation of 1780, and tells at length the story of Arnold's treason, its frustration by the capture of André and his pathetic fate. This "one romance of the Revolution" is a thrilling tale, and all adornment is given to it. The account of the struggle to save André's life gives the interest of controversy, as does the defense of Washington's course. The anecdote and the illustrative parallel are both supplied by the case of Captain Nathan Hale, executed by the English as an American spy. The address closes with a fitting tribute to André's three captors, whose modest monument marked the spot, and a very effective quotation of William of Orange's heroic oath at his coronation, "I will maintain."

OUTLINE OF SPEECH BY GOVERNOR FORAKER AT THE DEDICATION OF OHIO'S MONUMENT TO THE ANDREWS RAIDERS, AT CHATTANOOGA

Why this monument and this dedication. The story of the raid, the suffering of the raiders, and heroism of those who died.

The controversial part covered two points—the military value of the raid, and the manner in which the raiders had been treated by the enemy while prisoners.

The illustrative setting was the historic background of Chattanooga and the contrasts of war and peace.

OUTLINE OF ADDRESS BY CHAUNCEY M. DEPEW AT DINNER ON THE 70TH BIRTHDAY OF JOHN JAY

Not on the programme—pleasantry with Mr. Choate (President) about his railroad fees. Mr. Choate wants it made the rule for all ex-presidents of the club to have a dinner on their 70th birthday. This will help them to live at least that long, as Gladstone and Bismarck, when they had an object, have lived on in spite of the doctors!

Depew, a native of the same county as three generations of Jays. Services of the Revolutionary Jay.

The Anecdote.—General Sherman yesterday told a beautiful young girl— Generals always interested in beautiful young girls—that he would be willing to throw away all he was doing or had done to start at her time of life again. But the nation could not permit that, nor could it in the case of John Jay— closing words of tribute and esteem to the guest of the evening.

OUTLINE OF ADDRESS BY CHAUNCEY M. DEPEW AT THE RECEPTION TO HENRY M. STANLEY BY THE LOTUS CLUB

The speaker jests about his own locks whitened by the cares of railroading, and the raven hair of the reporters—where do they get their dye?

Stanley's lecture fee, $250.—Lotus Club gets one for only the price of a dinner!

Stanley a great artist in his descriptions as well as a great traveler.

Americans a nation of travelers.—This makes railroads prosperous! What some reporters have done.

The motive makes heroism.—Livingstone the missionary—his rescue by Stanley.

The civilized Africa of the future with Stanley for its Columbus.

SPEECHES AT A DINNER GIVEN TO THE RELIGIOUS PRESS

Toast.—"The Religious Press and Literature."

First, what are sound views of literature; second, what is a religious paper? The speaker used two illustrations bound in one. A great book is the Nilometer which measures intellectual life as the original Nilometer measured the life and fertility of the land of Egypt. A description of the rise of the Nile and of the *Divine Comedy* of Dante, as such a measurer of the life of the Middle Ages, made up the speech.

Toast.—"Religious Press and Questions of the Day."

Eternity begins *here*. The paper must show on which side of any question the right lies. It should go even further than this. It should cover a wider range of topics and aim to secure the attention of the general public to the questions it discusses and so entitle it to circulate more widely.

Toast.—"Should Religious Papers Make Money?"

If I may make the paying papers, anybody may make the others. Money losing—soon comes, *hic jacet*. Money making proves usefulness and renders the issue of a paper possible. Letter from the oldest editor of New York in which he says the editor is under life sentence to hard labor.

Toast.—"The Religious Paper and Scholarship."

He laments that he has no letter from an editor to read (like the last speaker), and tells a story of a Methodist, on request, praying for rain; and when a terrible storm came, the man who asked, was heard to murmur: "How these Methodists do exaggerate." This was to show the excellence of the dinner. Two other stories were used by the speaker, about the length and discursiveness of his talk. The people need and will read deep, accurate, and scholarly productions. There ought to be a general paper for such. Something has been done in that direction by two religious papers.

The speaker treated his topic by giving a semi-humorous review of the preceding speeches. He showed how denominational traits affected each item in the work of the paper. He did not make just the kind of a paper *he* liked best, for some people were of the same taste as Artemus Ward, who always ordered *hash* at a restaurant, because he then knew what he was getting! The speaker also referred ironically to the mistaken idea that church papers could not pay, and gave striking instances to the contrary. He concluded that denominational papers may be as successful in their line as those purely undenominational and independent.

RESPONSE TO THE TOAST, "THE NAVY: OUR COUNTRY'S BEST WALL OF DEFENSE"

1. The disasters which different ports of our country have experienced from invading forces during three great wars. No foe now on this continent which we need fear—our enemies, if any, will come by sea.

2. The defense by fortified harbors cannot be relied on, for when one place is defended another may be attacked, and the coast-line is so great that an unguarded spot may be found. But our glorious navy will seek the foe at any and every point.

3. Past glory of the Navy. Paul Jones in the Revolutionary War singeing John Bull's beard at his own fireside. 1812. The ships of iron that kept the Confederate States engirdled and forbade outside meddling with domestic troubles.

4. The Navy, by showing the world that we are impregnable, should be the best promoter of a solid peace.

RESPONSE TO THE TOAST, "GENERAL JACKSON: A DIAMOND IN THE ROUGH, BUT A DIAMOND"

1. The hero of New Orleans, though rough, was a strong and great man. Stories about him always popular. His indorsing State papers "O.K." when he approved them, and saying that these letters meant "*oll korrect*." The victor and the spoils.

2. His connection with great questions, such as the currency and nullification. Popularity with his own party.

3. Proved to be a great commander by the manner in which he used his very slender resources at the battle of New Orleans—the backwoods riflemen and the breastworks of cotton.

RESPONSE TO THE TOAST, "THE WORKING MAN: MAY HE LOVE HIS WORK AND HAVE PLENTY OF IT, WITH GOOD WAGES PROMPTLY PAID"

1. For a healthy man a reasonable amount of work is no misfortune, but a blessing. Idleness is a curse, and leads to all kinds of evil. (See story in Anecdote No. 21 at end of this volume—of the tramp who earned seventy-five cents and quit work because he feared that he could not bear the curse of riches! Not many of us have this kind of fear.)

2. Toil with pen and brain as real, and may be as exhausting as with the hand and foot.

3. But to defraud a workman of one cent of his earnings is a peculiarly atrocious crime. How this may be done indirectly. All persons who believe in this toast should deal justly and fairly, and try to hold others to the same rule.

4. The true workman wants work and fair play; not patronage and flattery, but sympathy and friendship.

A NOMINATING SPEECH

The great conventions that nominate candidates for the Presidency of the United States furnish examples on the largest scale of the nominating speech. But officers of societies of almost any character may be nominated in addresses that are very similar. The following outline of a speech of general character may be easily modified to suit any case in which such help is desired.

Mr. Chairman: It gives me great pleasure to place before you, the name of a candidate who is so well qualified and so fully deserving of this honor, and of every other, that may be conferred upon him, as ———. In giving him your votes, you can make no mistake. [Here state previous offices held, or trusts filled, or other evidences of fitness for the post in view.] In addition, I am happy to state that he represents [here name locality, section, class, or opinion, being careful to adduce only those which will be pleasing to the persons whose votes are sought.] On his behalf, I can promise faithful service, and the prompt discharge of every duty. Others may have as much zeal for the cause: some may have as long a training for the duties of this office; a few may possibly have as legitimate a claim upon any honors or rewards in your gift, but where else can you find such a combination of claims?

The illustrative anecdote will naturally be of the candidate himself, of his popularity, availability, or other good quality, or of some person or element strongly supporting him.

SPEECH ACCEPTING A NOMINATION

1. An honor of which any man must be deeply sensible as well as proud. The importance or high character of the body making the nomination.

2. The degree of surprise felt that the candidate should be preferred to so many worthy competitors. W by the honor is especially prized, and the reasons, if any; why the candidate would have preferred a different selection.

3. The motives which make him willing to bear the burdens entailed by this nomination.

4. The hope of being able to support his competitors for other offices, or other terms of this office.

5. With all his sense of unworthiness, the candidate dares not set up his judgment against that of the honorable body which has named him, for the office of ———, and he therefore bows to their decision and gratefully accepts the [unexpected?] honor conferred upon him. Should the people—not for his sake, but for the sake of the cause represented—have the intelligence and good judgment [of which there is not a shadow of doubt?] to indorse the nomination, he will exert all the power he possesses, to faithfully fill the position their choice has bestowed upon him.

SPEECH IN A POLITICAL CANVASS

No form of speech is so easy as a political address in a hot campaign. The people know enough of the general argument in advance, to appreciate a strong statement of it, or the addition of new items. They already have much of that interest in the theme that other classes of speakers must first seek to arouse. The tyro makes his feeble beginnings in the sparsely settled portions of the country, but the polished orator is welcomed by large audiences at the centres of population, and wins money, fame, and possibly a high office. Americans have many opportunities of hearing good speeches of this character, and not only become competent judges, but learn to emulate such examples.

1. A bright story, a personal incident, a local "hit," or, best of all, a quick, shrewd caricature of some feature of the opposing party, will gain attention and half win the battle. A speaker was once called upon to make an address after a political opponent had taken his seat. This man at one time strongly indorsed a measure to which his own party was bitterly opposed. The measure was defeated notwithstanding his opposition, and he was obliged to sanction his party's action. The audience being familiar with this, the speaker referred to it by saying: "Oh! *he* approves, does he! Imagine a kicked, cuffed, pounded, and dragged across a road, bracing himself at every step, but forced over at last and tied to a post; then imagine *that mule* straightening himself up and saying, 'Thank Heaven, we crossed that road, didn't we?' It was difficult to move the mule, he was obstinate, but it made no difference. My opponent was obstinate too, but what did it avail!"

2. The criticism of our opponents' platform or principles. Their fallacies, mistakes, and misrepresentations.

3. Their history. How they have carried out all their bad and dangerous doctrines, but have slurred over and allowed to drop out of sight their promises of good.

4. The contrast. Plain statement [and there is nothing more effective in a speech than a plain, dear, and condensed statement] of the opposing issues.

5. The man. [The personal element in a canvas nearly always overshadows political doctrine, except when a new party or new measure is rising into prominence.] Our men brilliant, able, safe. Our opponents the opposite. [Public character only should be criticized. Gossip, scandal, slander are abominable, and seldom well received by any audience. Poison, the assassin's dagger, and the spreading of infamous stories do not belong to honorable warfare.]

SPEECH AFTER A POLITICAL VICTORY. SELECTED

1. We are masters of the field. Completeness of victory [told in military language].

2. Sympathy for the defeated. We will treat their leaders with Good Samaritan generosity, but we invite the rank and file to enlist with us, unless they prefer to go home and pray for better luck next time.

3. Only by joining us can they get a nibble at the spoils. Probably they will, for many of them are men of seven principles—five loaves and two fishes. The "cohesive power of public plunder."

4. We must not be careless after victory, but reorganize, be vigilant, keep our powder dry. The "outs" are hungry, and an enemy will fight terribly for rations. "Brag is a good dog, but Holdfast is a better."

5. Now let us all rejoice over the defeat of a party many of whose members we respect personally, but which, as a whole, we regard as an immense nuisance.

SPEECH AFTER A POLITICAL DEFEAT. SELECTED

My Political Brethren: You seem to be in the dumps! Don't like the figures; wish they were a cunningly devised fable. How did it happen? Big vote and intolerable cheating cooked our goose. But we are india-rubber and steel springs, and no amount of hard usage can take the fight out of us.

Let our opponents laugh! We are not savage—would not hurt a hair of their heads personally, but politically will skin them alive next time. But we prefer to convert them, and hope they will hear our speakers as often as possible before the next election.

A CHAIRMAN'S OR PRESIDENT'S SPEECH

At a public meeting some one interested in the object for which it has convened calls the assembly to order. After securing attention he proposes the name of some person as chairman or president. When the nomination is seconded he takes the vote and announces the election. It will then be in order for the person chosen to take a position facing the assembly and to make a brief speech.

"Ladies and Gentlemen: I have no wish to disparage your judgment, although I think it might have been exercised to better advantage by electing some of the able persons I see before me. But I thank you for this honor, which I appreciate the more highly and accept the more readily because of say deep interest in the question of ——, which is now before us. First, however, please nominate a secretary."

When, however, the president or chairman elected is himself a prime mover in the business for which the meeting is called, it will be perfectly proper for him to extend his speech, upon accepting the chair, by stating clearly but briefly the object of the meeting; or, if he prefers, he may ask some one in whose powers of plausible and persuasive statement he has confidence to do this in his place. Formal argument is not advisable in the opening speech; but the best argument consists in giving a compact statement and ample information. In this way the cause may be half won by the chairman's speech or the speech of his proxy.

A GENERAL OUTLINE FOE ALL OCCASIONS

The Introduction. The speaker's modesty or inability, the lateness of the hour, the merit of preceding speeches, the literary treats that are to follow, the character of the dinner, personal allusion to the president or to the audience—*but not all of these in one address.*

The Discussion. Here refer to the toast or theme—be sure to put in a humorous anecdote. Make it as appropriate as possible, but don't fail to bring it in. Get up a short controversy: set up a man of straw if you can find nobody else, and then make an onslaught upon him; but *be sure he has no friends in the audience*!

Conclusion. A graceful compliment to some one, a reference to an expected speaker, or a word indicating the part of your subject of which you will not treat, or give a *very* quick summary of what you have already said.

ILLUSTRATIVE AND HUMOROUS ANECDOTES

With a number of the following anecdotes a few suggestions are given as to the manner in which they may be used. The habit of thinking how a good story may be brought into an address should be formed, after which these hints will be superfluous. At the outset they may help to form the habit.

1. INDEPENDENCE OF A MONOPOLY

[A good illustration of complete independence. It can be used as a humorous description of a monopoly or as a compliment to a man who has complete control of his own affairs.]

An inquisitive passenger on a railroad recently had the following dialogue:

"Do you use the block system on this road?" inquired the passenger.

"No, sir," replied the conductor, "we have no use for it."

"Do you use the electric or pneumatic signals?"

"No, sir."

"Have you a double track?"

"No."

"Well, of course, you have a train dispatcher, and run all trains by telegraph?"

"No."

"I see you have no brakeman. How do you flag the rear of your train if you are stopped from any cause between stations?"'

"We don't flag."

"Indeed! What a way to run a railroad! A man takes his life in his hand when he rides on it. This is criminally reckless!"

"See here, mister! If you don't like this railroad you can get off and walk. I am president of this road and its sole owner. I am also board of directors, treasurer, secretary, general manager, superintendent, paymaster, trackmaster, general passenger agent, general freight agent, master mechanic, ticket agent, conductor, brakeman, and boss. This is the Great Western Railroad of Kentucky, six miles long, with termini at Harrodsburg and Harrodsburg Junction. This is the only train on the road of any kind, and ahead of us is the only engine. We never have collisions. The engineer does his own firing, and runs the repair shop and round-house all by himself. He and I run this railway. It keeps us pretty busy, but we've always got time to stop and eject a sassy passenger. So you want to behave yourself and go through with us, or you will have your baggage set off here by the haystack!"

2. EXPLANATION

[To ridicule extravagant explanations that do not explain—or unreasonable pretensions to antiquity.]

An old Scotch lady, who had no relish for modern church music, was expressing her dislike to the singing of an anthem in her own church one day, when a neighbor said: "Why, that is a very old anthem! David sang that anthem to Saul." To this the old lady replied: "Weel, weel! I noo for the first time understan' why Saul threw his javelin at David when the lad sang for him."

3. RIDING A HOBBY

[To illustrate hobby-riding—very appropriate where many toasts and speeches run in one line.]

A boy in Buffalo, N. Y., who was asked to write out what he considered an ideal holiday dinner *ménu*, evolved the following:

Furst Corse.

Mince pie.

Second Corse.

Pumpkin pie and turkey.

Third Corse.

Lemon pie, turkey, and cranberries

Fourth Corse.

Custard pie, apple pie, chocolate cake and plum pudding.

Dessert.

Pie.

4. HOBSON'S CHOICE

[Suitable caricature for any one who tries to make merit of doing what he cannot help.]

"If my employer does not retract what he said to me this morning I shall leave his store." "Why, what did he say?" "He told me to look for another place."

5. WHEN TO BE SILENT

[A silent guest might tell this to show that he had found a way to be of greatest service at a banquet.]

Mrs. Penfield—"My husband has found a way by which he says I am of the greatest help to him in his literary work."

Mrs. Hillaire—"How nice that must be for you, my dear! But how are you able to do it?"

Mrs. Penfield—"As soon as I see him at his desk I go into another room and keep perfectly quiet until he has finished."

6. PAYING FOR YOUR WHISTLE

[Would be a good answer to one who gave a compliment, and tried in that way to shove off a speech or other duty upon the one complimented.]

McSwatters—"It's very funny."

Mrs. McSwatters—"What is?"

McSwatters—"Why, when the doctor treats me I always have to pay for it."

7. GOOSE-CHASE

[Would come in well after several had declined to speak, the goose being the one who finally consents and tells the story.]

A lady had been looking for a friend for a long time without success. Finally, she came upon her in an unexpected way. "Well," she exclaimed, "I've been on a perfect wild-goose chase all day long, but, thank goodness, I've found you at last."

8. THE PERPLEXED SAGE

[To show that the chairman may safely confide in his own power to manage such poor material as the person who tells the story assumes himself to be.]

"And now what is it?" asked the sage, as the young man timidly approached. "Pray, tell me," asked the youth, "does a woman marry a man because of her confidence in the man, or because of her confidence in her ability to manage him?" For once the sage had to take the question under advisement.

9. QUICK THOUGHT

[The following illustrates the advantages of a happy retort, the importance of a felicitous phrase, or of quick thought and ready speech. It might be said that the preceding speaker was as ready as:]

When Napoleon (then a student at Brienne) was asked how he would supply himself with provisions in a closely-invested town, he answered, without a moment's hesitation, "From the enemy," which so pleased the examiners that they passed him without further questions.

10. [The Russian General Suvaroff is said to have promoted one of his sergeants for giving substantially the same answer.]

The Emperor Paul, of Russia, was so provoked by the awkwardness of an officer on review that he ordered him to resign at once and retire to his estate. "But he has no estate," the commander ventured. "Then give him one!" thundered the despot, whose word was law, and the man gained more by his blunders than he could have done by years of the most skillful service.

11. [The anger of an actor took the same turn as that of the Czar.]

Colley Cibber once missed his "cue," and the confusion that followed spoiled the best passage of Betterton, who was manager as well as actor. He rushed behind the scenes in a towering passion, and exclaimed, "Forfeit, Master Colley; you shall be fined for such stupidity!" "It can't be done," said a fellow-actor, "for he gets no salary." "Put him down for ten shillings a week and fine him five!" cried the furious manager.

12. INSIGNIFICANT THINGS

[The need of accuracy, or how insignificant things sometimes change the meaning, is shown by the following.]

A merchant of London wrote his East India factor to send him 2 or 3 apes; but he forgot to write the "r" in "or," and the factor wrote that he had sent 80, and would send the remainder of the 2 0 3 as soon as they could be gathered in.

13. A very well-known writer had a similar experience. He was selling copies of his first literary venture, and telegraphed to the publisher to send him "three hundred books at once." He answered. "Shall I send them on an emigrant train, or must they go first-class? Had to scour the city over to get them. You must be going into the hotel business on a great scale to need so many Cooks." I was bewildered; but all was explained when a copy of the dispatch showed that the telegraph clerk had mistaken the small "b" for a capital "C."

14. MAKING AN EXCUSE; OR, JOHNNY PEEP

[A guest pleading to be excused from a speech or a song might say that he wanted to be accounted as "Johnny Peep" in the following story which Allan Cunningham tells of Robert Burns.]

Strolling one day in Cumberland the poet lost his friends, and thinking to find them at a certain tavern he popped his head in at the door. Seeing no one there but three strangers, he apologized, and was about to retire, when one of the strangers called out, "Come in, Johnny Peep." This invitation the convivial poet readily accepted, and spent a very pleasant time with his newly-found companions. As the conversation began to flag, it was proposed that each should write a verse, and place it, together with two-and-six pence, under the candlestick, the best poet to take the half-crowns, while the unsuccessful rhymers were to settle the bill among them. According to Cunningham, Burns obtained the stakes by writing:

"Here am I, Johnny Peep;

I saw three sheep,

And these three sheep saw me.

Half-a-crown apiece

Will pay for their fleece,

And so Johnny Peep goes free."

15. STERN LOGIC

[Probably this boy would have seen the necessity of avoiding such rich banquets as this.]

"Say, ma, do they play base-ball in heaven?"

"Why, no, my dear; of course not. Why do you ask?"

"Huh! Well, you don't catch me being good and dying young then; that's all."

16. MISTAKEN BREVITY

["Brevity is the soul of wit;" and calculation and economy are very commendable; but they may be carried to extremes. This may be used when the last speaker has closed a little abruptly.]

This is the message the telegraph messenger handed a young man from his betrothed "Come down as soon as you can; I am dying. Kate."

Eight hours later he arrived at the summer hotel, to be met on the piazza by Kate herself.

"Why, what did you mean by sending me such a message?" he asked.

"Oh!" she gurgled, "I wanted to say that I was dying to see you, but my ten words ran out, and I had to stop."

17. CHARITY BEGINS AT HOME

Breslau, a celebrated juggler, being at Canterbury with his troupe, met with such bad success that they were almost starved. He repaired to the church wardens, and promised to give a night's takings to the poor if the parish would pay for hiring a room, etc. The charitable bait took, the benefit proved a bumper, and the next morning the church wardens waited upon the wizard to touch the receipts. "I have already disposed of dem," said Breslau; "de profits were for de poor. I have kept my promise, and given de money to my own people, who are de poorest in dis parish!"

"Sir!" exclaimed the church wardens, "this is a trick."

"I know it," replied the conjurer; "I live by my tricks."

18. CHARITY; OR, A GOOD WORD FOR EVERY ONE—EVEN THE DEVIL.

[It is well to feel charitably and kindly at all times, but especially at a dinner party.]

A friend said to a Scotchman who was celebrated for possessing these amiable qualities, "I believe you would actually find something to admire in Satan himself." The canny Scot replied, "Ah! weel, weel, we must a' admit, that auld Nick has great energy and perseverance."

[If the chairman has been very persistent in calling out reluctant speakers, the foregoing would be a good story to turn the laugh upon him.]

19. INGENIOUS REASON

[The Scotchman referred to in the last anecdote was as ingenious in finding a reason as the boy mentioned in the following:]

"Can you suggest any reason why I should print your poem?" said the overbearing editor.

The dismal youth looked thoughtful, and then replied:

"You know I always inclose a stamp for the return of rejected manuscript?"

"Yes."

"Well, if you print it you can keep the stamp."

20. AMBIGUITY OF WORDS

[The equivocal use of words in our language.]

Recently a west-bound train on the Fitchburg (Mass.) Railroad had just left the town of Athol When the conductor noticed among the new passengers a young man of intelligent appearance. He asked for the young man's fare, and the latter handed him a ticket to Miller's Falls and with it a cent. For a moment the conductor suspected a joke, but a look at the passenger's face convinced him to the contrary.

"What is this cent for?" the conductor asked.

"Why, I see," answered the young fellow, "that the ticket isn't good unless it is stamped, and as I don't happen to have a stamp with me I give you the cent instead. You can put it on, can't you?"

The good-natured conductor handed back the coin with a smile, remarking that it was a small matter, and he would see that it was all right.

21. USELESS REGRET

[Persons who pretend to regret something without making a real effort to better it are hit off by this anecdote.]

A father called his son rather late in the morning, and finding him still abed, indignantly demanded: "Are you not *ashamed* to be caught asleep this time of day?"

"Yes, rather," returned the ingenious youth, "but I'd ruther *be ashamed* than git up."

22. NO HAPPINESS IN WEALTH

[The great advantage of being fully adapted to one's situation and contented with it.]

There are people who cannot hold their heads under the influence of sudden riches. They immediately begin to degenerate. They have become so used to humble circumstances that wealth is a curse. Here is a case:

A tramp, for some mysterious reason, had accepted an offer to work about the place, for which he was to receive his meals, sundry old clothes, and 25 cents a day in cash. For the first two or three days he did very well, and he was paid 50 cents on account. He did not spend the money, but he began to grow listless and sad, and at the end of the week he interviewed his employer.

"You've been very kind to me, sir," he said, "and I want to thank you for what you have done."

"That's all right," was the reply. "I'm glad to be able to help you."

"I know that, sir, and I appreciate it, but I shall have to give it all up, sir."

"What's that for? Don't I pay you enough?"

"Oh! yes, sir; that isn't it. I have 75 cents left, sir, but I find that money doesn't bring happiness, sir, and I guess I'll resign and go back to the old ways, sir. Wealth is a curse to some people, sir, and I fancy I belong to that class. Good-bye, sir." And he shambled off down the path and struck the highway.

23. SHORT BUT POINTED

[Splendid for a speaker called up rather late in the evening—even if he should make a short speech afterward.]

Being nobody in particular, a Mr. Bailey was placed last on the list of the speakers. The chairman introduced several speakers whose names were not on the list, and the audience were tired out when he said, "Mr. Bailey will now give you his address."

"My address," said Mr. Bailey, rising, "is No. 45 Loughboro Park, Brixton Road, and I wish you all good night."

24. REASONING IN A CIRCLE

[This is very common, as in the case of the heroine of this story.]

The director of a Chicago bank tells how his wife overdrew her account at the bank one day last month. "I spoke to her about it one evening," said he, "and told her she ought to adjust it at once. A day or two afterward I asked her if she had done what I suggested. 'Oh! yes,' she answered. 'I attended to that matter the very next morning after you spoke about it. I sent the bank my check for the amount I had overdrawn.'"

25. EXTREME ECONOMY

[Economy is a great virtue, but it should not be extreme.]

An old lady of Massachusetts was famed in her native township for health and thrift. To an acquaintance who was once congratulating her upon the former she said:

"We be pretty well for old folks, Josiah and me. Josiah hasn't had an ailin' time for fifty years, 'cept last winter. And I ain't never suffered but one day in my life, and that was when I took some of the medicine Josiah had left over, so's how it shouldn't be wasted."

26. SENSIBLE TO THE LAST

[How we commend those who take our standards and help us.]

A story is told of a late Dublin doctor, famous for his skill and also his great love of money. He had a constant and profitable patient in an old shopkeeper in Dame Street. This old lady was terribly rheumatic and unable to leave her sofa. During the doctor's visit she kept a £1 note in her hand, which duly went into Dr. C.'s pocket. One morning he found her lying dead on the sofa. Sighing deeply, the doctor approached, and taking her hand in his, he saw the fingers closed on his fee. "Poor thing," he said as he pocketed it, "sensible to the last."

27. FISHING FOR A COMPLIMENT

[Fishing for compliments is sometimes dangerous.]

A well-known Congressman, who was a farmer before he went into politics, was doing his district not long ago, and in his rambles he saw a man in a stumpy patch of ground trying to get a plow through it. He went over to him, and after a brief salutation he asked the privilege of making a turn or two with the plow. The native shook his head doubtfully as he looked at his visitor's store clothes and general air of gentleman of elegant leisure, but he let him take the plow. The Congressman sailed away with it in fine style, and plowed four or five furrows before the owner of the field could recover his surprise. Then he pulled up and handed the handles over to the original holder.

"By gravy, mister," said the farmer, admiringly, "air you in the aggercultural business?"

"No," laughed the statesman.

"Y'ain't selling plows?"

"No."

"Then what in thunder air you?"

"I'm the member of Congress from this district."

"Air you the man I voted for and that I've been reading about in the papers doin' legislatin' and sich in Washington?"

"Yes."

"Well, by hokey, mister," said the farmer, as he looked with admiration over the recently-plowed furrows, "ef I'd a had any idea that I was votin' fer a waste of sich good farmin' material I'd voted fer the other candidate as shore as shootin'."

28. BEYOND EXPRESSION

[When called on for a speech one may answer the chairman in the words of this lady:]

She was in her room when some people came to call. Her husband received the company, and after awhile said to his daughter, who was playing about the room:

"Go up-stairs and tell your mamma that Mr. and Mrs. Blank have come to call."

The child went, and after a while returned and began to play again.

"Did you tell your mamma that Mr. and Mrs. Blank are here?" asked the father.

"Oh! yes."

"And what did she say?"

The little girl looked up, and after a moment's hesitation, exclaimed:

"She said—well, she said, 'O dear!'"

29. THE TOAST OF THE EVENING

[The comment upon this incident by the editor is not less amusing than the speech.]

It is not always a pleasant thing to be called upon suddenly to address a public meeting of any sort, as is amusingly illustrated by the following speech at the opening of a free hospital by one who was certainly not born an orator:

"Gentlemen—ahem—I—I—I rise to say—that is, I wish to propose a toast, which I think you'll all say—ahem—I think, at least, that this toast is, as you'll say, the toast of the occasion. Gentlemen, I belong to a good many of these things, and I say, gentlemen, that this hospital requires no patronage—at least, what I mean is, you don't want any recommendation. You've only got to be ill—got to be ill."

"Now, gentlemen, I find by the report" (turning over the leaves in a fidgety way) "that from the year seventeen—no eighteen—no, ah, yes, I'm right—eighteen hundred and fifty—no, it's a '3'—thirty-six—eighteen hundred and thirty-six, no less than one hundred and ninety-three millions—no! ah!" (to a committeeman at his side) "Eh? oh, yes, thank you—yes—one hundred and ninety-three thousand—two millions—no" (after a close scrutiny at the report) "two hundred and thirty-one—one hundred and ninety-three thousand, two hundred and thirty-one! Gentlemen, I beg to propose—success to this admirable institution!"

To what the large and variously stated figures referred no one in the audience ever felt positive, but all agreed, as he had said they would, that this was the toast of the evening.

30. BEE LINE

[He knew how to escape from more than one kind of fire.]

A soldier on guard in South Carolina during the war was questioned as to his knowledge of his duties.

"You know your duty here, do you, sentinel?"

"Yes, sir."

"Well, now, suppose they should open on you with shells and musketry, what would you do?"

"Form a line, sir."

"What! one man form a line?"

"Yes, sir; form a bee-line for camp, sir."

31. VENTRILOQUISM

["Take the good the Gods provide."]

At Raglan Castle, said Mr. Ganthony, the ventriloquist, I gave an entertainment in the open air, and throwing my voice up into the ivy-covered ruins, said: "What are you doing there?"

To my amazement a boy answered: "I climbed up 'ere this mornin' just to see the folk and 'ear the music; I won't do no harm."

I replied: "Very well, stay there, and don't let any one see you, do you hear?"

The reply came: "Yes, muster, I 'ear."

This got me thunders of applause. I made up my mind to risk it, so I bowed, and the boy never showed himself.

32. A SLIGHT MISTAKE

[Orders should be strictly obeyed.]

A celebrated German physician, according to a London paper, was once called upon to treat an aristocratic lady, the sole cause of whose complaint was high living and lack of exercise. But it would never have done to tell her so. So his medical advice was:

"Arise at five o clock, take a walk in the park for one hour, then drink a cup of tea, then walk another hour, and take a cup of chocolate. Take breakfast at eight."

Her condition improved visibly, until one fine morning the carriage of the baroness was seen to approach the physician's residence at lightning speed. The patient dashed up to the doctor's house, and on his appearing on the scene she gasped out:

"O doctor! I took the chocolate first!"

"Then drive home as fast as you can," directed the astute disciple of Æsculapius, rapidly writing a prescription, "and take this emetic. The tea must be underneath."

The grateful patient complied. She is still improving.

33. PRESENCE OF MIND

[A fine story to illustrate the value (money value) of presence of mind.]

A witty person whom Bismarck was commissioned by the Emperor to decorate with the Iron Cross of the first class, discomfited the Chancellor's attempt to chaff him. "I am authorized," said Bismarck, "to offer you one hundred thalers instead of the cross." "How much is the cross worth?" asked the soldier. "Three thalers." "Very well, then, your highness, I'll take the cross and ninety-seven thalers." Bismarck was so surprised and pleased by the ready shrewdness of the reply that he gave the man both the cross and the money.

34. JOKE ON A DUDE

[A good story for one who has some power of personation, for the dudes get little sympathy.]

A crowded car ran down the other evening. Within was a full-blown, eye-glassed, drab-gaitered dude, apparently satisfied that he was jammed in among an admiring community. On the rear platform a cheery young mechanic was twitting the conductor and occasionally making a remark to a fresh passenger. Everybody took it in good part as a case of inoffensive high spirits, all but the dude, who evinced a strong disgust.

When the young man called out to an old gentleman, "Sit out here, guvinor, on the back piazza," or to another, "Don't crowd there; stay where the breezes blow," the dude looked daggers, and at last, grabbing the conductor's elbow and indicating the young man by a nod of the head, evidently entered a protest. Every one saw it. So did the young man, and he gathered his wits together like a streak to finish that dude. He did it all with an imperturbable good humor and seriousness which would carry conviction to the most doubting.

"Well, I never!" he began, poking his head inside the doorway with an air of comic surprise. "Jes' to see you a-sitting there, dressed up like that. Catch on to them gaiters, will you? Ain't you got the nerve to go up and down Broadway fixed up like that, and your poor father and mother workin' hard at home? Ain't you 'shamed o' yourself, and your father a honest, hard-workin' driver, and your mother a decent, respectable washwoman? Y' ain't no good, or you wouldn't have gev up your place, and I think I'll go look after it myself and put a decent man in it."

He stepped off the car as if bent on doing this at once, and the dude, unable to resist the ridicule of the situation or defend the attack, hastily stepped off after him.

35. NEWSPAPER REPORTER

[Equally good for a missionary meeting or a gathering of newspaper men.]

A young journalist was requested to write something about the Zenana Mission. He assured the readers of the paper that among the many scenes of missionary labor, none had of late attracted more attention than the Zenana Mission, and assuredly none was more deserving of this attention. Comparatively few years had passed since Zenana had been opened up to British trade, but already, owing to the devotion of a handful of men and women, the nature of the inhabitants had been almost entirely changed. The Zenanese, from being a savage people, had become, in a wonderfully short space of time, practically civilized; and recent travelers to Zenana had returned with the most glowing accounts of the continued progress of the good work in that country. He then branched off into the "laborer-worthy-of-his-hire" side of this great work, and the question was aptly asked if the devoted laborers in that remote vineyard were not deserving of support. Were civilization and Christianity to be snatched from the Zenanese just when both were within their grasp? So on for nearly half a column the writer meandered in the most orthodox style, just as he had done scores of times before when advocating certain missions. Some one who found him the next day running his finger down the letter Z, in the index to the "Handy Atlas," with a puzzled look upon his face, knew he had had a letter from the editor.

36. HOW A WOMAN PROPOSED

[A variation of the old and always pleasing theme.]

They were dining off fowl in a restaurant. "You see," he explained, as he showed her the wishbone, "you take hold here. Then we must both make a wish and pull, and when it breaks the one who has the bigger part of it will have his or her wish granted." "But I don't know what to wish for," she protested. "Oh! you can think of something," he said. "No, I can't," she replied; "I can't think of anything I want very much." "Well, I'll wish for you," he exclaimed. "Will you, really?" she asked. "Yes." "Well, then, there's no use fooling with the old wishbone," she interrupted, with a glad smile, "you can have me."

37. LUCKY ANSWER

[Certainly Thompson would be a lawyer, ready for any emergency.]

In times past there was in a certain law school an aged and eccentric professor. "General information" was the old gentleman's hobby. He held it as incontrovertible that if a young lawyer possessed a large fund of miscellaneous knowledge, combined with an equal amount of common sense, he would be successful in life. So every year the professor put on his examination papers a question very far removed from the subject of criminal law. One year it was, "How many kinds of trees are there in the college yard?" the next, "What is the make-up of the present English cabinet?"

Finally the professor thought he had invented the best question of his life. It was, "Name twelve animals that inhabit the polar regions." The professor chuckled as he wrote this down. He was sure he would "pluck" half the students on that question and it was beyond a doubt that that opprobrious young loafer Thompson would fail. But when the professor read the examination papers, Thompson, who had not answered another question, was the only man who had solved the polar problem. This was Thompson's answer: "Six seals and six polar bears." Thompson got his degree with distinction.

38. DOUBLE EDUCATION

A young doctor, wishing to make a good impression upon a German farmer, mentioned the fact that he had received a double education, as it were. He had studied homoeopathy, and was also a graduate of a "regular" medical school. "Oh! dot vas noding," said the farmer, "I had vonce a calf vot sucked two cows, and he made nothing but a common schteer after all."

39. REMNANTS

[This and the preceding have a little spice of ill-nature, and while enjoyable must be applied carefully.]

Wife—"Such a dream as I had last night, dear!"

Husband—"May I hear about it?"

"Well, yes; I dreamed I was in a great establishment where they sold husbands. They were beauties; some in glass cases and marked at fearful prices, and others were sold at less figures. Girls were paying out fortunes, and getting the handsomest men I ever saw. It was wonderful."

"Did you see any like me there, dear?"

"Yes; just as I was leaving I saw a whole lot like you lying on the remnant counter."

40. INDIRECT AND DIRECT

[The following instances show that it is necessary to heed indirect as well as direct meanings.]

Mr. Callon, M. P. for Louth, Ireland, a stanch opponent of the Sunday Closing and Permissive Bill and personally a great benefactor to the Revenue, replying to the Irish Attorney-General, said: "The facts relied on by the learned gentleman are very strange. Now, Mr. Speaker, *I swallow a good deal.*

['Hear, hear,' 'Quite true,' 'Begorra, you can,' and roars of laughter.] I repeat, *I can swallow a great deal* ['Hear, hear,' and fresh volleys of laughter], but I can't swallow that." A few nights before, in a debate which had to do with the Jews, Baron de Worms had just remarked, "*We owe much to the Jews*," when there came a feeling groan from a well-known member in his back corner, "*We do*."

41. AN UNMARRIED MAN'S WIFE

At a dinner at Delmonico's, after the bottle had made its tenth round, one of the company proposed this toast: "To the man whose wife was never vixenish to him!" A wag of an old bachelor jumped up and said: "Gentlemen, as I am the only *unmarried* man at this table, I suppose that that toast was intended for me."

42. A DILEMMA

"I am no good unless I strike," said the match. "And you lose your head every time you do strike," said the box.

43. COURAGEOUS GIRL

[The following is a good instance of an elaborate story and a sharp retort.]

It is not always safe to presume upon the timidity or ignorance of folks. The most demure may be the most courageous. A gentleman who attempted to play a practical joke in order to test the courage of a servant, was nonplused in a very unexpected way. Here is his story:

I am very particular about fastening the doors and windows of my house. I do not intend to leave them open at night as an invitation to burglars to enter. You see, I was robbed once in that way last year, and I never mean to be again; so when I go to bed I like to be sure that every door and window is securely fastened.

Last winter my wife engaged a big, strong country girl, and the new-comer was very careless about the doors at night. On two or three occasions I came down-stairs to find a window up or the back door unlocked. I cautioned her, but it did her no good. I therefore determined to frighten her. I got some false whiskers, and one night about eleven o'clock I crept down the back-stairs to the kitchen, where she was. She had turned down the gas, and was in her chair by the fire fast asleep, as I could tell by her breathing, but the moment I struck a match she awoke.

I expected a great yelling and screaming, but nothing of the sort took place. She bounced out of her seat with a "You villain!" on her lips, seized a chair by the back, and before I had made a move she hit me over the head, forcing me to my knees. I tried to get up, tried to explain who I was, but in vain.

Before I could get out of the room she struck me again, and it was only after I had tumbled up the back-stairs that she gave the alarm. Then she came up to my room, rapped at the door, and coolly announced:

"Mr. ——, please get up. I've killed a burglar."

44. MORAL SUASION

"What are your usual modes of punishment?" was among the questions submitted to a teacher in rural district in Ohio. Her answer was, "I try moral suasion first, and if that does not work I use capital punishment."

As it was a neighborhood where moral suasion had not been a success, and the children were scarce the committee took no risks.

45. CUTE BOY

The teacher in geography was putting the class through a few simple tests:

"On which side of the earth is the North Pole?" he inquired.

"On the north side," came the unanimous answer.

"On which side is the South Pole?"

"On the south side?"

"Now, on which side are the most people?"

This was a poser, and nobody answered. Finally, a very young scholar held up his hand.

"I know," he said, hesitatingly, as if the excess of his knowledge was too much for him.

"Good for you," said the teacher, encouragingly; "tell the class on which side the most people are."

"On the outside," piped the youngster, and whatever answer the teacher had in her mind was lost in the shuffle.

46. PERPLEXED

Bob—"Hello! I'm awfully glad to see you!" Dick—"I guess there must be some mistake. I don't owe you anything, and I am not in a condition to place you in a position to owe me anything!"

47. BEN FRANKLIN'S OYSTERS

Benjamin Franklin was not unlike other boys in his love for sophomoric phrases. It is related that one day he told his father that he had swallowed some acephalus molluscus, which so alarmed him that he shrieked for help. The mother came in with warm water, and forced half a gallon down

Benjamin's throat with the garden pump, then held him upside down, the father saying, "If we don't get those things out of Bennie he'll be poisoned sure." When Benjamin was allowed to get his breath he explained that the articles referred to were oysters. His father was so indignant that he whipped him for an hour for frightening the family. Franklin never afterward used a word with two syllables when a monosyllable would do.

48. FAMILY AFFAIRS

"Newlywed seems to find particular delight in parading his little family affairs before the eyes of his acquaintances," "Does he? What are they? Scandals?" "Nop, twins."

49. A BURGLAR'S EXPERIENCE

A New York paper prints this extract from the reminiscences of a retired burglar:

"I think about the most curious man I ever met," said the retired burglar, "I met in a house in eastern Connecticut, and I shouldn't know him, either, if I should meet him again unless I should hear him speak. It was so dark where I met him that I never saw him at all. I had looked around the house down-stairs, and actually hadn't seen a thing worth carrying off. It was the poorest house I ever was in, and it wasn't a bad-looking house on the outside, either. I got up-stairs and groped around a little, and finally turned into a room that was darker than Egypt. I had not gone more than three steps in this room when I heard a man say:

"'Hello, there.'

"'Hello,' says I.

"'Who are you?' says the man; 'burglar?'

"And I said yes; I did do something in that line occasionally.

"'Miserable business to be in, ain't it?' said the man. His voice came from a bed over in the corner of the room, and I knew he hadn't even sat up.

"And I said, 'Well, I dunno. I got to support my family some way.'

"'Well, you've just wasted a night here,' says the man. 'Did you see anything down-stairs worth stealing?'

"And I said no, I hadn't.

"'Well, there's less up-stairs,' says the man; and then I heard him turn over and settle down to go to sleep again. I'd like to have gone over there and kicked him, but I didn't. It was getting late, and I thought, all things considered, that I might just as well let him have his sleep out.'"

50. HITTING A LAWYER

"Have you had a job to-day, Tim?" inquired a well-known legal gentleman of the equally well-known, jolly, florid-faced old drayman, who, rain or shine, summer or winter, is rarely absent from his post.

"Bedad, I did, sor."

"How many?"

"Only two, sor."

"How much did you get for both?"

"Sivinty cints, sor."

"Seventy cents! How in the world do you expect to live and keep a horse on seventy cents a day?"

"Some days I have half a dozen jobs, sor. But bizness has been dull to-day, sor. On'y the hauling of a thrunk for a gintilman for forty cints an' a load av furniture for thirty cints; an' there was the pots an' the kittles, an' there's no telling phat; a big load, sor."

"Do you carry big loads of household goods for thirty cents?"

"She was a poor widdy, sor, an' had no more to give me. I took all she had, sor; an' bedad, sor, a lyyer could have done no better nor that, sor."

51. CUTTING SHORT A PRAYER

Many a spiritual history is condensed into a miniature in the following:

Two fishermen—Jamie and Sandy—belated and befogged on a rough water, were in some trepidation lest they should never get ashore again. At last Jamie said:

"Sandy, I'm steering, and I think you'd better put up a bit of a prayer."

Sandy said: "I don't know how."

Jamie said: "If you don't I'll just chuck ye overboard."

Sandy began: "O Lord, I never asked onything of Ye for fifteen year, and if Ye'll only get us safe back I'll never trouble Ye again."

"Whist, Sandy," said Jamie, "*the boat's touched shore; don't be beholden to onybody.*"

52. UNREMITTING KINDNESS

Jerrold was asked if he considered a man kind who remitted no funds to his family when away. "Oh! yes. *Unremitting kindness*," said he.

53. AMUSING BLUNDER

One of the passengers on board the ill-fated "Metis" at the time of the disaster was an exceedingly nervous man, who, while floating in the water, imagined how his friends would acquaint his wife of his fate. Saved at last, he rushed to the telegraph office and sent this message: "Dear P——, I am saved. *Break it gently to my wife.*"

54. COMPLIMENT TO A LADY

[How nicely this might fit into a ladies' party.]

Sidney Smith, the cultivated writer and divine, who, when describing his country residence, declared that he lived twelve miles from a lemon, was told by a beautiful girl that a certain pea in his garden would never come to perfection. "Permit me then," said he, taking her by the hand, "*to lead perfection to the pea.*"

55. TOO SLIM

[The great evil of mixing religion and politics are well set forth in the following incident:]

"Gabe," said the governor to an old colored man, "I understand that you have been ousted from your position of Sunday-school superintendent."

"Yes, sah, da figured aroun' till da got me out. II was all a piece of political work, though; and I doan see why de law of de lan' doan prevent de Sunday-schools an' churches from takin' up political matters!"

"How did politics get you out?"

"Yer see, some time ago, when I was a candidate for justice ob de peace, I gin' a barbecue ter some ob my frien's. De udder day da brung up de fack an' ousted me."

"I don't see why the fact that you gave a barbecue to your friends should have caused any trouble."

"Neider does myse'f, boss; but yer see da said dat I stole de hogs what I barbecued. De proof wa'nt good, an' I think dat da done wrong in ackin' upon sech slim testimony. Da said dat I cotch de hogs in a corn fid'. I know dat wan't true, 'case it was a wheat fid' whar I cotch 'em."

56. A FAST-DAY TOAST

On one of the fast-days—a cold, bleak one, too—Father Foley, a popular and genial priest, on his way from a distant visitation, dropped in to see Widow O'Brien, who was as jolly as himself, and equally as fond of the creature comforts, and, what is better, well able to provide them. As it was about dinner-time, his reverence thought he would stay and have a "morsel" with the old dame; but what was his horror to see served up in good style a pair of splendid roast ducks!

"Oh! musha, Mistress O'Brien, what have ye there?" he exclaimed, in well-feigned surprise.

"Ducks, yer riverence."

"Ducks! roast ducks! and this a fast-day of the holy Church!"

"Wisha! I never thought of that; but why can't we eat a bit of duck, yer riverence?"

"Why? Because the Council of Trint won't lave us—that's why."

"Well, well, now, but I'm sorry fur that, fur I can only give ye a bite of bread and cheese and a glass of something hot. Would that be any harrum, sir?"

"Harrum! by no manes, woman. Sure we must live any way, and bread and cheese is not forbid!"

"Nayther whiskey punch?"

"Nayther that."

"Well, thin, yer riverence, would it be any harrum fur me to give a toast?"

"By no manes, Mrs. O'Brien. Toast away as much as ye like, bedad!"

"Well, thin, *here's to the Council of Trint, fur if it keeps us from atin', it doesn't keep us from drinkin'*!"

57. THE SUN STANDING STILL

James Russell Lowell, when concluding an after-dinner speech in England, made a happy hit by introducing the story of a Methodist preacher at a camp-meeting, of whom he had heard when he was young. He was preaching on Joshua ordering the sun to stand still: "My hearers," he said, "there are three motions of the sun; the first is the straightforward or direct motion of the sun, the second is the retrograde or backward motion of the sun, and the third is the motion mentioned in our text—'the sun stood still.' Now, gentlemen, I do not know whether you see the application of that story to after-dinner oratory. I hope you do. The after-dinner orator at first begins and goes straight forward—that is the straightforward motion of the sun; next he goes back and begins to repeat himself a little, and that is the retrograde or backward motion of the sun; and at last he has the good sense to bring himself to an end, and that is the motion mentioned in our text of the sun standing still."

58. NEUTRALIZING POISON

Col. John H. George, a New Hampshire barrister, tells a good story on himself. Meeting an old farmer recently whom he had known in his youth, the old fellow congratulated the Colonel on his youthful appearance.

"How is it you've managed to keep so fresh and good-looking all these years?" quoth he.

"Well," said George, "I'll tell you. I've always drank new rum and voted the Democratic ticket."

"Oh! yes," said the old man, "*I see how it is; one pizen neutralizes the other!*"

59. GENERAL BUTLER AND THE SPOONS

While General Butler was delivering a speech in Boston during an exciting political campaign, one of his hearers cried out: "How about the spoons, Ben?" Benjamin's good eye twinkled merrily as he looked bashfully at the audience, and said: "Now, don't mention that, please. *I was a Republican when I stole those spoons.*"

60. MAKING MOST OF ONE'S CAPITAL

[One should always make the most of his capital, as this orator did.]

"Fellow-citizens, my competitor has told you of the services he rendered in the late war. I will follow his example, and I shall tell you of mine. He basely insinuates that I was deaf to the voice of honor in that crisis. The truth is, I acted a humble part in that memorable contest. When the tocsin of war summoned the chivalry of the country to rally to the defense of the nation, I, fellow-citizens, animated by that patriotic spirit that glows in every American's bosom, hired a substitute for that war, and the bones of that man, fellow-citizens, now lie bleaching in the valley of the Shenandoah!"

61. MEETING HALF-WAY

[But the following man could get even more out of an unpromising situation.]

"Now, I want to know," said a man whose veracity had been questioned by an angry acquaintance, "just why you call me a liar. Be frank, sir; for frankness is a golden-trimmed virtue. Just as a friend, now, tell me why you called me a liar."

"Called you a liar because you are a liar," the acquaintance replied.

"That's what I call frankness. Why, sir, if this rule were adopted over half of the difficulties would be settled without trouble, and in our case there would have been trouble but for our willingness to meet each other half-way."

62. UNFORTUNATE MISTAKE

Judge ——, who is now a very able Judge of the Supreme Court of one of the great States of this Union, when he first "came to the bar," was a very blundering speaker. On one occasion, when he was trying a case of replevin, involving the right of property to a lot of hogs, he addressed the jury as follows:

"Gentlemen of the jury, there were just twenty-four hogs in that drove—just twenty-four, gentlemen—*exactly twice as many as there are in that jury-box!*" The effect can be imagined.

63. TAKEN AT HIS WORD

A pretentious person said to the leading man of a country village, "How would a lecture by me on Mount Vesuvius suit the inhabitants of your village?" "Very well, sir; very well, indeed," he answered; "a lecture by you on Mount Vesuvius would suit them a great deal better than a lecture by you in this village."

64. BRAGGING VETERANS

In warning veterans against exaggerating, a gentleman at a Washington banquet related the following anecdote of a Revolutionary veteran, who, having outlived nearly all his comrades, and being in no danger of contradiction, rehearsed his experience thuswise: "In that fearful day at Monmouth, although entitled to a horse, I fought on foot. With each blow I severed an Englishman's head from his body, until a huge pile of heads lay around me, great pools of blood on either side, and my shoes were so full of the same dreadful fluid that my feet slipped beneath me. Just then I felt a touch upon my shoulder, and, looking up, who should I behold but the great and good Washington himself! Never shall I forget the majesty and dignity of his presence, as, pressing his hand upon me, he said, 'My young friend, restrain yourself, and for heaven's sake do not make a slaughter-house of yourself.'"

65. EXCHANGING MINDS

Heinrich Heine, the German poet, apologizing for feeling dull after a visit from a professor said: "I am afraid you find me very stupid. The fact is, Dr. —— called upon me this morning, and *we exchanged our minds.*"

66. BUYING A LAWYER

[The willingness to pay full value for an article is a trait of character always appreciated.]

Lawyer B—— called at the office of Counselor F——, who has had considerable practice in bankruptcy, and said: "See here, F——, I want to know what the practice is in such and such a case in bankruptcy."

F——, straightening himself up and looking as wise as possible, replied: "Well, Mr. B——, I generally get paid for telling what I know."

B—— put his hand into his pocket, drew forth half a dollar, handed it to F——, and said: "Here, tell me *all* you know, and *give me the change.*"

67. WOULD NOT SAVE IT

In the old town of W——, in the Pine-tree State, lived one of those unfortunate lords of creation who had, in not a very long life, put on mourning for three departed wives. But time assuages heart-wounds, as well as those of the flesh. In due time a fourth was inaugurated mistress of his heart and house. He was a very prudent man, and suffered nothing to be wasted. When the new mistress was putting things in order, while cleaning up the attic she came across a long piece of board, and was about launching it out of the window, when little Sadie interposed, and said: "Oh! don't, mamma! *that is the board papa lays out his wives on, and he wants to save it!*" Nevertheless, *out it went.*

68. WIDOW OUTWITTED

In a Western village a charming, well-preserved widow had been courted and won by a physician. She had children. The wedding-day was approaching, and it was time the children should know they were to have a new father. Calling one of them to her, she said: "Georgie, I am going to do something before long that I would like to talk about with you."

"Well, ma, what is it!"

"I am intending to marry Dr. Jones in a few days, and—"

"Bully for you, ma! *Does Dr. Jones know it?*"

Ma caught her breath, but failed to articulate a response.

69. TOO KIND

[Where can we find a more touching manifestation of mutual benevolence than the following.]

In New Jersey reside two gentlemen, near neighbors and bosom friends, one a clergyman, Dr. B——, the other a "gentleman of means" named Wilson. Both were passionately fond of music, and the latter devoted many of his leisure hours to the study of the violin. One fine afternoon our clerical friend was in his study, deeply engaged in writing, when there came along one of those good-for-nothing little Italian players, who planted himself under his study window, and, much to his annoyance, commenced scraping away on a squeaky fiddle. After trying in vain for about fifteen minutes to collect his scattered thoughts, the Doctor descended to the piazza in front of the house, and said to the boy:

"Look here, sonny, you go over and play awhile for Mr. Wilson. Here is ten cents. He lives in that big white house over yonder. He plays the violin, and likes music better than I do."

"Well," said the boy, taking the "stamp," "*I would, but he just gave me ten cents to come over and play for you!*"

70. NOT FOOLED TWICE

San Francisco boasts of a saloon called the Bank Exchange, where the finest wines and liquors are dispensed at twenty-five cents a glass, with lunches thrown in free. A plain-looking person went in one morning and called for a brandy cocktail, and wanted it *strong*. Mr. Parker, as is usual with him, was very considerate, and mixed the drink in his best style, setting it down for his customer. After the cocktail had disappeared the man leaned over the bar and said that he had no change about him then, but would have soon, when he would pay for the drink. Parker politely remarked that he should have mentioned the fact before he got the drink; when his customer remarked: "I tried that on yesterday morning with one of your men, but he would not let me have the whiskey, so you could not play that dodge on me again!" This was too good for Parker, and he told the customer he was welcome to his drink, and was entitled to his hat in the bargain, if he wanted it.

71. BITING SARCASM

Standing on the steps at the entrance to one of the grand hotels at Saratoga, a young gentleman, in whom the "dude" species was strongly developed, had been listening with eager attention to the bright things which fell from the lips of the well-known wit and orator, Emory A. Storrs.

At last our exquisite exclaimed: "Er—Mr. Storrs,—I—er—wish, oh! how I—er—*wish*! that I had your—er—cheek."

Mr. Storrs instantly annihilated him with: "It is a most fortunate dispensation of Providence that you have not. For, *with my cheek and your brains*, you would be kicked down these steps in no time!"

72. INCORRIGIBLE NEIGHBOR

A lady in California had a troublesome neighbor, whose cattle overrun her ranch, causing much damage. The lady bore the annoyance patiently, hoping that some compunction would be felt for the damage inflicted. At last she caught a calf which was making havoc in her garden, and sent it home with a child, saying, "Tell Mrs. A. that the calf has eaten nearly everything in the garden, and I have scarcely a cabbage left."

The feelings of the injured lady may be imagined when she received this reply: "The cabbage nearly all eaten! Well, I must get over and borrow some before it is all gone!"

73. DISGUSTED OFFICER

Some years since a party of Indians drove off all the live-stock at Fort Lancaster. A few days afterward Captain —— was passing through the post, and stopped a couple of days for rest. While there an enthusiastic officer took him out to show him the trail of the bad Indians, how they came, which way they went, etc. After following the trail for some distance the Captain turned to his guide and exclaimed: "Look here; if you want to find any Indians, you can find them; *I haven't lost any*, and am going back to camp."

74. IRATE PRISONER

A man arrested for stealing chickens was brought to trial. The case was given to the jury, who brought him in guilty, and the judge sentenced him to three months' imprisonment. The jailer was a jovial man, fond of a *smile*, and feeling particularly good on that particular day, considered himself insulted when the prisoner looking around his cell told him it was dirty, and not fit for a hog to be put in. One word brought on another, till finally the jailer told the prisoner if he did not behave himself he would put him out. To which the prisoner replied: "I will give you to understand, sir, I have as good a right here as you have!"

75. TRUTHFUL PRISONER

The eccentric old King of Prussia, father of Frederick the Great, while visiting the Potsdam prison, was much interested in the professions of innocence the prisoners made. Some blamed their conviction on the prejudice of judges; others, upon the perjury of witnesses or the tricks of bad companions. At length he accosted a sturdy, closely-fettered prisoner with the remark, "I suppose you are innocent, too."

"No, your Majesty," was the unexpected response. "I am guilty, and richly deserve all I get."

"Here, you turnkey," thundered the monarch, "come and turn out this rascal, quick, before he corrupts this fine lot of innocent and abused people that you have about you."

76. RULING PASSION

There are persons now living in Bennington who remember old Billy B——, of whom it might be said he furnished an example of the "ruling passion strong in death." When very ill, and friends were expecting an early demise, his nephew and a man hired for the occasion had butchered a steer which had been fattened; and when the job was completed the nephew entered the sick-room, where a few friends were assembled, when, to the astonishment of all, the old man opened his eyes, and turning his head slightly, said, in a full voice, drawing out the words:

"What have you been doing?"

"Killing the steer," was the reply.

"What did you do with the hide?"

"Left it in the barn; going to sell it by-and-by."

"Let the boys drag it around the yard a couple of times; it will make it weigh heavier."

And the good old man was gathered unto his fathers.

77. BAD SPECULATION

[This is told of bears, rattlesnakes, etc., as well as Indians.]

At a recent festive occasion a gentleman who was making a few remarks was repeatedly interrupted by another one of the company. He bore it patiently at first, but finally said that it reminded him of a story he had heard. He said that a man, whom business had called away a short distance from his home in the city, thought he would pay his way back again by purchasing a number of hogs and driving them home. He did so, but when he and the hogs arrived at their destination the market for the latter had fallen considerably in price, and the hogs had also lost weight on the journey. It was remarked to him that he had made rather a bad speculation. "Yes—well, yes," he answered reflectively. "Yes—but then, you see, *I had their company all the way!*"

78. SATISFIED WITH HIS SITUATION

[The following may not be strictly true, but it well illustrates that there is always a lower depth in misfortune, and—that Western roads are often somewhat muddy.]

Some years ago, when riding along one of the almost impassable roads in the far West, I observed a dark-looking object lying in the middle of the road, and my natural curiosity impelled me to dismount and examine it. It proved to be a hat, somewhat muddy and dilapidated, but emphatically a hat. On lifting it up, to my surprise I found that it covered a head—a human head—which protruded sufficiently out of the mud to be recognizable as such. I ventured to address the evidently wide-awake head, and remarked that it seemed to be in a pretty bad sort of a fix.

"Wa'al, yes!" the lips replied; "you're about right thar, stranger; *but then I ain't anyway near as bad off as the horse that's under me!*"

79. A GOOD WORD FOR THE DEVIL

A conference preacher one day went into the house of a Wesleyan Reformer, and saw the portraits of three expelled ministers suspended from the walls.

"What!" said he, "have you got them hanging there?"

"Oh! yes," was the answer; "they are there."

"Ah! well; but one is wanted to complete the set."

"Pray, who is that?"

"Why, the devil, to be sure."

"Ah!" said the Reformer, "but he is not yet expelled from the Conference."

80. MARRYING A WIDOW

In Cadiz, Ohio, a preacher was summoned to the hotel to make an expectant couple one. In the course of the preliminary inquiries the groom was asked if he had been married before, and admitted that he had been—three times. "And is this lady a widow," was also asked, but he responded promptly and emphatically, "No, sir; *I never marry widows.*"

81. A GOOD SALE

Several years ago there resided in Saratoga County a lawyer of considerable ability and reputation, but of no great culture, who had an unusually fine taste in paintings and engravings—the only evidence of refinement he ever exhibited. A clergyman of the village in which he lived, knowing his fondness for such things, introduced to him an agent of a publishing house in the city who was issuing a pictorial Bible in numbers. The specimen of the style of work exhibited to the lawyer was a very beautiful one, and he readily put down his name for a copy. But in the progress of the publication the character of the engravings rapidly deteriorated, much to the disgust of the enlightened lawyer. The picture of Joseph, very indifferently done, provoked him beyond endurance, and seizing several of the numbers he sallied forth to reproach the parson for leading him into such a bad bargain. "Look at these wretched scratches," said he, turning the pages over, "and see how I have been imposed upon! Here is a portrait of Joseph, whom his brethren sold to the Egyptians for twenty pieces of silver; and let me tell you, parson, *if Joseph looked like that it was a mighty good sale!*"

82. TRIUMPHS OF MEDICINE

A priest was called upon by a superstitious parishioner, who asked him to do something for her sick cow. He disclaimed knowing anything about such matters, but could not put her off. She insisted that if he would only say some words over the cow, the animal would surely recover. Worn out with importunity, he seized his book in desperation, walked around the four-legged patient several times, repeating in a sonorous voice the Latin words, which mean, "If you die, you die; and if you live, you live," and rushed off disgusted. But the woman was delighted, and sooth to say the cow quickly recovered.

But in time the good man himself was taken sick, and grew rapidly worse. His throat was terribly swollen, and all medical aid was exhausted. The word passed around the parish that the priest must die. When Bridget heard the peril of her favorite pastor she was inspired by a mighty resolve. She hurried to the sick-room, entered against the protest of the friends who were weeping around, and with out a word to any one with her strong hands dragged his reverence's bed to the middle of the floor, and with the exact copy of his very gestures and voice marched around the bed, repeating the sonorous and well-remembered Latin phrase, "If you die, you die; and if you live, you live." The priest fell into a fit of uncontrollable laughter, and in his struggle for breath and self-control the gathering in his throat broke and his life was saved!

Mighty are the triumphs of medicine!

83. TIT FOR TAT

An old fellow in a neighboring town, who is original in all things, especially in excessive egotism, and who took part in the late war, was one day talking to a crowd of admiring listeners, and boasting of his many bloody exploits, when he was interrupted by the question:

"I say, old Joe, how many of the enemy did you kill during the war?"

"How many did I kill sir? *how many* enemies did I kill? Well, I don't know just 'zactly *how* many; but I know this much—I killed as many o' them *as they did o' me*!"

84. SLEEPING ON TOP

During a homeward trip of the "Henry Chauncey," from Aspinwall, the steerage passengers were so numerous as to make them uncomfortable. As for sleeping accommodation, it was aptly described by a Californian, who approached the captain, and said:

"I should like to have a sleeping-berth, if you please."

"Why, where have you been sleeping these last two nights since we left?"

"Wa'al, I've been sleeping a-top of a sick man; *but he's better now, and won't stand it no longer!*"

85. SAMBO AND THE LAWYER

In a Macon (Ga.) court the other day a lawyer was cross-examining a negro witness, and was getting along fairly well until he asked the witness what his occupation was. "I'se a carpenter, sah." "What kind of a carpenter?" "They calls me a jackleg carpenter, sah." "What is a jackleg carpenter?" "He is a carpenter who is not a first-class carpenter, sah." "Well, explain fully what you understand a jackleg carpenter to be," insisted the lawyer. "Boss, I declare I dunno how ter splain any mo' 'cept to say hit am jes' the same difference 'twixt you an' a fust-class lawyer."

86. SIXTY-CENT NAP

On board a train in the West an eccentric preacher wanted a sleeping-berth, but had only sixty cents, while the lowest price was a dollar. Naturally he did not get on very fast with the porter; but after wearing out the patience of that functionary in vain efforts to stretch the sixty cents, the conductor was sent for. All proposals to borrow, to pledge an old Waterbury watch, and other financial expedients failed; but the circle was squared when the preacher said, "I'll lie down, and *when I have slept sixty cents worth, you send that bed-shaker to rout me out.*" The procession started for the sleeper amid the hilarity of the passengers, but the tradition is that he slept the whole night through and far into the morning.

87. PREFERRED TO WALK

A great traveler once found himself on the shore of the Sea of Galilee. He was at once beset by boatmen, who wanted to take him out to sail on the waters where Christ had walked. He yielded to their importunities, and returned to the shore in about an hour. But his devout meditations were greatly disturbed when he was told that the charge was $10. With energy he declared that it was robbery, that it was not worth so much to sail all over their little lake, and demanded, "What makes you charge so dreadfully?" "Why," said the innocent boatman, "because dese ese de lake were de Saviour walked on de water." "Walked! walked! did He? Well, if the boatmen of that day charged as you fellows do, I should think He *would* walk."

88. HORACE GREELEY'S JOKE

On one occasion a person, who wished to have a little fun at the expense of his constituency, said in a group where Horace Greeley was standing: "Mr. Greeley and I, gentlemen, are old friends. We have drunk a good deal of brandy and water together." "Yes," said Mr. Greeley, "that is true enough. You drank the brandy, and I drank the water."

89. DOCTORS AND DEADHEADS

Fifty years ago the principal avenue of Detroit had a toll-gate close to the entrance of the Elmwood Cemetery road. As this cemetery had been laid out some time previous to the construction of the plank road, it was arranged that all funeral processions should be allowed to pass along the latter toll-free. One day as a well-known physician stopped to pay his toll, he observed to the gate-keeper:

"Considering the benevolent character of our profession, I think you ought to let physicians pass free of charge."

"No, no, doctor," replied the man; "we can't afford that. You send too many 'deadheads' through here as it is."

The story traveled, and the two words became associated.

90. BOOMING A TOWN

They tell a story of a man who came into Omaha one day, and wanted to trade his farm for some city lots. "All right," replied the real-estate agent, "get into my buggy, and I'll drive you out to see some of the finest residence sites in the world—water, sewers, paved streets, cement sidewalks, electric light, shade trees, and all that sort of thing," and away they drove four or five miles into the country. The real-estate agent expatiated upon the beauty of the surroundings, the value of the improvements made and projected, the convenience of the location, the ease and speed with which people who lived there could reach town, and the certainty of an active demand for such lots in the immediate future. Then, when he was breathless, he turned to his companion, and asked:

"Where's your farm?"

"We passed it coming out here," was the reply. "It's about two miles nearer town."

91. ATHLETIC NURSE

Young Wife—"Why, dear, you were the stroke oar at college, weren't you?"

Young Husband—"Yes, love."

"And a prominent member of the gymnastic class?"

"I was leader."

"And quite a hand at all athletic exercises?"

"Quite a hand? My gracious! I was champion walker, the best runner, the head man at lifting heavy weights, and as for carrying—why, I could shoulder a barrel of flour and—"

"Well, love, just please carry the baby for a couple of hours, I'm tired."

92. TOO PREMATURE

[Anything rather premature may be illustrated by the following:]

A spring bird that had taken time by the forelock flew across the lawn near this city one day last week. His probable fate is best described in this pathetic verse, author unknown:

"The first bird of spring

Essayed for to sing;

But ere he had uttered a note

He fell from the limb,

A dead bird was him,

The music had friz in his throat."

93. A BEWILDERED IRISHMAN

The poet Shelley tells an amusing story of the influence that language "hard to be understood" exercises on the vulgar mind. Walking near Covent Garden, London, he accidentally jostled against an Irish navvy, who, being in a quarrelsome mood, seemed inclined to attack the poet. A crowd of ragged sympathizers began to gather, when Shelley, calmly facing them, deliberately pronounced:

"I have put my hand into the hamper, I have looked on the sacred barley, I have eaten out of the drum. I have drunk and am well pleased. I have said, 'Knox Ompax,' and it is finished."

The effect was magical, the astonished Irishman fell back; his friends began to question him. "What barley?" "Where's the hamper?" "What have you been drinking?" and Shelley walked away unmolested.

94. OBEYING ORDERS

When General Sickles, after the second battle of Bull Run, assumed command of a division of the Army of the Potomac, he gave an elaborate farewell dinner to the officers of his old Excelsior Brigade.

"Now, boys, we will have a family gathering," he said to them, as they assembled in his quarters. Pointing to the table, he continued: "Treat it as you would the enemy."

As the feast ended, an Irish officer was discovered by Sickles in the act of stowing away three bottles of champagne in his saddle-bags.

"What are you doing, sir," gasped the astonished General.

"Obeying orders, sir," replied the captain, in a firm voice: "You told us to treat the dinner as we would the enemy, and you know, General, what we can't kill we capture."

95. A SPEECH FROM THE REAR PLATFORM

An Irish street-car conductor called out shrilly to the passengers standing in the aisle:

"Will thim in front plaze to move up, so that thim behind can take the places of thim in front, an' lave room for thim who are nayther in front nor behind?"

96. A WAY OUT OF IT

"What's the matter with you," asked a gentleman of a friend whom he met. "You looked puzzled and worried."

"I am," said the friend. "Maybe you can help me out"

"Well, what is it?"

"I am subject at intervals," said the friend, "to the wildest craving for beefsteak and onions. It has all the characteristics of a confirmed drunkard's craving for rum. This desire came upon me a few minutes ago, and I determined to gratify it. Then suddenly I remembered that I had promised to call this evening on some ladies, and I must keep that promise. Yet my stomach is shouting for beefsteak and onions, and I am wavering between duty and appetite."

"Can't you wait until after the call?" asked the gentleman, solicitously.

"Never," said the friend, earnestly.

"Can't you postpone the call?"

"Impossible," declared the friend.

"Well," said the gentleman, "I'll tell you what to do: go to John Chamberlin's café; order your beefsteak and onions, and eat them. When you get your bill it will be so big that it will *quite take your breath away*."

97. THE EXTENT OF SCIENCE

"And now," said the learned lecturer on geology who had addressed a small but deeply attentive audience at the village hall, "I have tried to make these problems, abstruse as they may appear, and involving in their solution the best thoughts, the closest analysis, and the most profound investigations of our noblest scientific men for many years; I have tried, I say, to make them seem comparatively simple and easily understood, in the light of modern knowledge. Before I close this lecture I shall be glad to answer any questions that may occur to you as to points that appear to need clearing up or that may have been overlooked."

There was a silence of a few moments, and then an anxious-looking man in the rear of the hall rose up.

"I would take it as a favor," he said, "if you could tell me whether science has produced as yet any reliable and certain cure for warts."

98. WHAT'S IN A NAME?

One of the managers of a home for destitute colored children tells a funny story about the institution. She went out there to see how things were getting along, and found a youngster as black as the inside of a coal mine tied to a bed-post, with his hands behind him.

"What is that boy tied up there for?" she demanded of the attendant.

"For lying, ma'am. He is the worstist, lyingest nigger I ever seen."

"What's his name?

"George Washington, ma'am," was the paralyzing reply.

99. STILL ROOM FOR RESEARCH

"What is this new substance I hear so much about?" asked the eminent scientist's wife.

"What new substance, my dear?"

"The element in the air that has just been detected."

"Oh! that, my dear," he answered, beaming over his spectacles with the good nature of superior wisdom, "is known as argon!"

"Oh!"

"Yes; its discovery is one of the most remarkable triumphs of the age. It has revolutionized some of the old theories, or at least it will revolutionize them before it gets through."

"What is it?"

"It's—er—a—did you say, what is it?"

"I said that."

"Well—ahem—you see, we haven't as yet discovered much about it except its name."

100. HE WAS "'PISCOPAL"

An Episcopal clergyman passing his vacation in Indiana met an old farmer who declared that he was a "'Piscopal."

"To what parish do you belong?" asked the clergyman.

"Don't know nawthin' 'bout enny parish," was the answer.

"Well, then," continued the clergyman, "what diocese do you belong to?"

"They ain't nawthin' like that 'round here," said the farmer.

"Who confirmed you, then?" was the next question.

"Nobody," answered the farmer.

"Then how are you an Episcopalian?" asked the clergyman.

"Well," was the reply, "you see it's this way: Last winter I went down to Arkansas visitin', and while I was there I went to church, and it was called 'Piscopal, and I he'rd them say 'that they left undone the things what they'd oughter done and they had done some things what they oughten done,' and I says to myself, says I: 'That's my fix exac'ly, and ever since I considered myself a 'Piscopalian."

The clergyman shook the old fellow's hand, and laughingly said:

"Now I understand, my friend, why the membership of our church is so large."

101. JOHNNY'S EXCUSE

A little girl brought a note to her school-teacher one morning, which read as follows. "Dear teacher, please excuse Johnny for not coming to school today. He is dead." Johnny was excused.

Milton Keynes UK
Ingram Content Group UK Ltd.
UKHW010706240424
441619UK00004B/313